San Salvador

Cabrillo's Galleon of Discovery

Bruce Linder

A Special Publication of

MAINS'L HAUL

A Journal of Pacific Maritime History

Vol. 48: 1 & 2 Winter/Spring 2012

Maritime Museum of San Diego
San Diego, California

Published by

Maritime Museum of San Diego
1492 North Harbor Drive
San Diego, California 92101

Published in the United States of America

10 9 8 7 6 5 4 3 2 1

Cataloging in Publication Data

Linder, Bruce R., 1949-
    San Salvador: Cabrillo's galleon of discovery / Bruce R. Linder.
       p. cm.
    Includes bibliographical references and index.
    ISBN: 0-944380-31-9 (paperback)

    1. San Salvador (Ship) 2. Shipbuilding–Spain–History–16th
century. 3. Cabrillo, Juan Rodriguez, d. 1543.
4. California–Discovery and Exploration–Spanish.
5. California–History–To 1846, I. Title.

VM299.7.M6 2011   623.8/21/0972–dc23   2011915009

Printed by Crest Offset Printing Company, San Diego, California
Design by Enyedy Graphics, San Diego, California
Production by the Maritime Museum of San Diego, California

Table of Contents

Introduction – 6

1. Spritsail
2. Fore Topsail
3. Foresail
4. Main Topsail
5. Mainsail
6. Lateen

Foreword
by Dr. Ray Ashley

How did California begin?

It certainly began long ago, well before recorded history, with astonishing geologic and tectonic movements and with widespread migrations and settlement of early peoples. But the true beginning of the world's awareness of California and, just as important, the beginning of California's remarkable tradition of multi-cultural growth, began at the exact same hour – on September 28, in the year 1542.

On this prominent date, the sturdy Spanish galleon *San Salvador* entered San Diego Bay and her captain, Juan Rodríguez Cabrillo, claimed the bay and the surrounding country for Spain, "in the name of the Emperor our Lord, King of Castille." From this day, four centuries ago, California's modern history began, and from this day everything that had been before changed.

At the center of this new beginning stood three small ships of the Spanish crown, the largest of which was a merchant galleon of about one-hundred feet in length. *San Salvador* and her consorts were more than conveyances. They formed the cresting wave of an unprecedented maritime expansion that would, for the first time, link all the peoples of the earth, branches of humanity that had been, for tens of thousands of years, separated by impassible oceanic barriers. As she probed the farthest reaches of her known world, she also represented the furthest reach of humanity's earliest large-scale technological system.

Today we are awash in large-scale technological systems such as the railroad, automobile, aircraft, radio, television and the internet. Transportation and communication have been broken into countless channels, but in the day when the oceanic sailing ship reigned supreme, it stood as the sole global channel in which people, things, information, and political power all moved together in the same package.

On September 28, 1542, *San Salvador* sailed at the frontier of the greatest exchange of plants, animals, technologies, germs, genes, belief systems, and economic activity that has ever transpired. We live in the aftermath of that exchange today, a pale and technologically placid projection of those truly revolutionary times. But, in that moment, she was the harbinger of a world that none of her crew could have imagined, much less thought inevitable. The only human adversary she had to fear was another of her own kind, and none more formidable were to be found in the entire breadth of the Pacific Ocean. *San Salvador* enjoyed but a brief time on the world stage, but in the flash of her confrontation with the unknown, a unique coincidence of time, place, and attributes rendered her the most powerful object within her entire world.

The story of how *San Salvador* came to be and how she made her way up a challenging and unknown coastline is an epic story in itself.

To historically depict and accurately interpret this unique moment in both California and American history, a replica *San Salvador* has risen from the shore of that same San Diego Bay. She is as close in design as one can make a ship of her era today. To fully understand *San Salvador*, the gallant Juan Rodríguez Cabrillo, or Californians of 1542, one must first begin with a comprehensive and accurate written history (as Bruce Linder has done so well here), and then carefully step from the shore and proceed onboard this fine ship. For it is only then that one can experience what Cabrillo and his crew felt four hundred and seventy years ago: the heave of the deck underfoot, the music of the breeze through the rigging, and the magic of a distant and unfamiliar coastline rising from the horizon in the first hint of daylight.

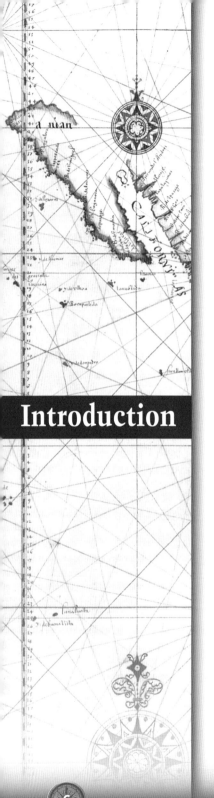

Introduction

*N*orthward, 1542. Basking in the gentle warmth of a late summer morning and churning through filigrees of spindrift on an aquamarine sea, a galleon of Spain reigned supreme in her ocean world. Except for her two small consorts, following her every move like faithful hounds, no other ocean-going vessel of either commerce or discovery plied the same seas for over fifteen-hundred miles in any direction. No vessel other than *San Salvador*.

Faraway to starboard, a bleak and lonely shoreline spanned the entire horizon. As distant as one could see, the land stood dirty brown and barren with occasional manzanita, chaparral, or sagebrush. Far in the distance, sierras rose, stark and sharp-edged. Closer along the shoreline, salt marshes and coastal dunes caught the eye.

Those aboard *San Salvador* called the shore "California," as those three decades earlier had named a new offshore land thought to be an island. But *San Salvador* had seen no evidence of an island, no change in the coastline, no end of land, no northern limit to "California." This noble ship of Spain sailed cautiously northward, the land on her starboard side. Mountain by mountain, beach by beach, the terrain slipped past on a steady line leading north-by-northwest.

At nearly 100 tons in modern units, *San Salvador* was not the largest of her type, but stood as one of the major achievements of shipbuilding on the Pacific coast. She was solidly built, proven, and reliable – the favorite of her owner and master, Juan Rodríguez Cabrillo. On this day, all sails were drawing in the stiff breeze, the cross of Burgundy fluttered from the main truck and the colorful banner of the owner flew astern.

San Salvador had sailed from the frontier port of Navidad in New Spain, on June 27, 1542. Cabrillo's motivation was one of fame, which would come from exploration and discovery, and fortune, the dream of all seamen seeking riches at the end of their bowsprit. Cabrillo was confident and competent, a successful businessman, conquistador and risk-taker well attuned to the "affairs of the sea," and one of the richest men of New Spain.

Sailing up the coast of Mexico, *San Salvador* then crossed open ocean to reach the bold vistas of Cabo San Lucas at the very tip of the long California peninsula. The coast held few surprises; Cabrillo had brought copies of current charts and at least one member of his crew had sailed on a previous expedition along this same coast. After seven additional weeks

Bronze sculpture of the galleon *San Salvador* **on display at Cabrillo National Monument.**

Courtesy Cabrillo National Monument

San Salvador ◆ Cabrillo's Galleon of Discovery

of northward sailing, though, *San Salvador* had reached the farthest extent of previous discovery. There, the paper trace of the shoreline on the chart ended, and the land and sea areas beyond stood eerily blank on the textured vellum.

Coastal detail may have been lacking on *San Salvador's* chart, but several cartographers had already offered an outline of a broader picture of the Pacific. In 1542, most charts of the South Sea (as the Pacific Ocean was called) suggested an ocean perhaps only one-third its true breadth. One notable chart of the time had placed the islands of Japan quite close to California, about the same distance away from the California coast as a trip from California to Navidad in southern New Spain. The theory of 1542 surmised that the coast of California would bend dramatically westward to connect with the Asian continent. By sailing northward and closely following the California coast, one would ultimately reach the treasured Orient – a magnificent and enchanting goal.

So, as *San Salvador* faced the immediate challenge of navigating up a strange coastline, many thought that her voyage would end in the Orient and the Spice Islands of Southeast Asia. Nothing, though, would be easy. The sea terrified all. The ocean was the home of

Right: This portion of a worldwide map, by French cartographer Nicholas Sanson, was drawn in 1656 and shows the original concept of California as an island lying off the North American coast and the potential for a strait far to the north that would connect the Atlantic and Pacific – notions that were in constant discussion during Cabrillo's era. Noteworthy are depictions of mainland New Spain, the location of Native tribes and details along the California Pacific coast including the Channel Islands.
MMSD Map and Chart Collections

fabled monsters of the deep and deadly serpents.
Huge waves and terrifying winds ruled this watery
realm and once away from land the ships of men were
completely at its mercy. For sailors, until they had
flung their fragile vessel into the teeth of the unknown,
until they had explored the land and sea, and until
they had interacted with the peoples of their journey,
there would be surprises – rarely would these
"surprises" be good.

On September 28, 1542, *San Salvador* passed three
dry and uninhabited islands near the California
coastline. Lookouts high in the masts alerted the

"San Salvador had arrived at a port that the Spanish would call San Miguel. It was a 'surprise' for sure during a voyage of discovery, but it also would become a singular event that would echo down through history."

crew to a bold, wooded headland rising on the near horizon. The day was clear and other landmarks were also spied: "broad valleys... mountains further inland," and smoke from many small fires. The point of land was high and rugged, a finger of land pointing seaward.

From the direction of their advance, the lookouts would not have seen the tremendous prize that lay tucked just beyond the surfline. Rather, all attention was focused on the safety and security that the high headland might provide. It was *San Salvador's* practice to seek protected anchorages each night. The official narrative of the voyage reported that the ship covered only six leagues of distance (about fifteen and one-half nautical miles) that day, an indication that she faced a stiff headwind. The headland would have drawn them as a magnet toward it. But, as *captain-general* Cabrillo anchored his ships safely behind this great promontory, a stunning sight suddenly opened ahead: an "enclosed harbor which was very good," stretching as far as one could see.

San Salvador had arrived at a port that Cabrillo would name "San Miguel" after the feast day of St. Michael and his fleet's smallest vessel. It was a spectacular surprise, even for a voyage of discovery that would echo throughout history. For over the next three centuries, the mere presence of this "enclosed harbor which was very good" would continue to draw others, would figure in the strategies of nations, and would eventually influence the drawing of boundaries for the realms of men.

San Salvador's milestone discovery marks the founding date, in the European sense, for a new land and, in San Diego history, for a European outpost on the Pacific Ocean. As historian Dr. Ray Ashley wrote: "What was significant was that the small *San Salvador* would push the world's awareness of the mysterious, provocative and inspiring California coastline ahead. It established a point of origin for the evolution of everything that would later be recognized as California, and that perspective is as important to the study of history as, perhaps, any other critical milestone." All societies cherish a tale of their origin and *San Salvador* gives California its own, starting in San Diego Bay. This date, September 28, 1542, marks the first encounter between Europeans and California's Native Americans and the origin of California's proud history of multi-cultural diversity.

San Salvador was a moving island of Spanish culture advancing through uncharted seas and sailing passed a wilderness never before seen by Europeans. Her daily observations and entries in the log tell a story of peoples and land that were unique, fascinating, and complex. It also tells a tale of cultures that would begin to change that very day, the very moment the ship's log was opened and the very minute the ink was dry in its telling. Native traditions would capture this moment as well, with sagas of "first contact" and of what Europeans had brought to their land. *San Salvador* would turn the page of California history and open an era that would be vastly different from anything that had transpired for thousands of years before.

San Salvador ◆ *Cabrillo's Galleon of Discovery*

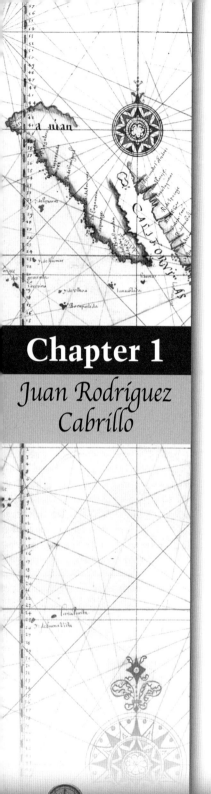

Chapter 1

Juan Rodríguez Cabrillo

he saga of the *San Salvador* begins with the man who conceived her, built her, owned her, trained her crew, tested her seaworthiness, and captained her as she sailed over the horizon to realize her destiny.

The historic record, stretching back some five centuries, has not been kind to this captain of *San Salvador*, Juan Rodríguez Cabrillo. Even today, there is much more unknown about this intrepid explorer than known...and much more assumed than proven.

It is not that historians haven't tried. Documents from the historical archives of New Spain and the Spanish court have been carefully translated and dissected, while fact-finding treks have been launched to cities (large and small) in Guatemala, Spain, and Portugal. Many records are missing or never existed and there are great gaps in our understanding of the life, stature, dreams and ambitions of this important figure in history.

The word "enigmatic" fits Cabrillo in the sense that his life is a puzzle. Facts about Cabrillo's life are fuzzy, and many of his accomplishments in historical archives are ambiguous or open to fundamental questions by researchers. No known picture or painting of Cabrillo exists. His writings are meager.

The traces of his name in official records are often only clues from his times rather than factual statements.

A fine statue of Cabrillo stands high atop the windswept promontory of Point Loma at the place where San Diego Bay joins the Pacific. The statue's location could not be better, standing at the exact juncture of the northward voyage where California began – in geography, in history and in perspective. There are parts of this artistic rendering of Cabrillo that are questionable: a coat of arms of the Kingdom of Portugal, for instance, and a broadsword, much more useful at a knight's roundtable than on the pitching decks and close confines of mariners. We know that no image of Cabrillo has survived in history for a sculptor to cast, so this famous statue represents his stature rather than replicates it. In this sense, it is extraordinary.

The Point Loma statue captures a personality and the spirit of a man,

No painting of Juan Rodríguez Cabrillo is known to exist, but sculptor Alvaro de Bree originally produced this 14-foot heroic sandstone statue in 1939 as a gift to the State of California. It commemorates Cabrillo and overlooks San Diego Bay.

Courtesy Cabrillo National Monument

largely unknown to history, in a manner that does superb justice to his accomplishments. Here, we see inner strength, stature, and a face that resonates toughness, determination, and presence. Looking at the statue, there is no doubt that this man is in command.

As important is the sculptor's work that surrounds Cabrillo with a balanced triangle of three icons: a cross, a set of navigation instruments, and a sword. This conveys a sense of harmony between a man and the realities of the world in which he lived. It is also a discerning clue to the make-up of the man himself: sailor, conquistador, explorer and man of faith.

To understand Juan Rodríguez Cabrillo, one must appreciate that he was a self-made man. The ticket to success in sixteenth-century Spain invariably involved family prerogative – noble standing, family connections, or status in the royal court. Of these advantages, Cabrillo had none.

No record exists of Cabrillo's birth. Several historians have suggested that he may have been born in Cuéllar, in north-central

Explorer of
California
1542

29
USA

Juan Rodríguez
CABRILLO

Spain, and moved later to Seville. Equally vague, Cabrillo never mentioned his parents nor where his parents came from, even when he was required to do so in official documents. This is highly unusual given the Spanish devotion to family heritage and strong regional identity. Cabrillo researchers point to this as a strong indicator of a humble origin or a disrupted upbringing. This may also indicate a father of unknown or shameful character.

As often seen in history, a young man of modest upbringing can frequently excel by gaining training in arms and journeying to a far frontier. This was certainly the case for a young Juan Rodríguez Cabrillo, reaching out to seek his fortune. His life began in the historical telling with his arrival in Santo Domingo on the large West Indies island of Hispaniola in 1509, or 1510, at the age of 12. Cabrillo's grandson later said under oath that Cabrillo came to the New World from Spain into the army of Pánfilo de Narváez. Cabrillo is often spoken of as Portuguese. This assumption first came from an annotation by Spanish Indies

An example of a common metal helmet used by Spanish conquistadors during the sixteenth and seventeenth centuries in the Americas.

Courtesy Museo del Carmen, Santiago de Chile

historian Antonio de Herrera y Tordesillas that referred to Cabrillo, seventy years after his death, as "Juan Rodríguez Cabrillo, Portuguese." Few historians today support this view, some indicating that the reference amounts only to an obscure printing or reference error that occurred far in the past. Portuguese historian Celestino Soares believes that Herrera may have pointed to Portuguese ancestry on Cabrillo's mother's side using complicated naming conventions of the day.

There is no question, though, that the service of Spain entirely absorbed Cabrillo's career. He always signed his name Juan Rodríguez in the Spanish manner rather than *João Rodrigues Cabrilho* in Portuguese. Cabrillo, a Spanish surname, was unknown as a surname in Portugal. Nearly everyone in the historical record treated him as a Spaniard: those in government, friends, and family – even his enemies.

There is great uncertainty where the name "Cabrillo" comes from and what it signifies. Cabrillo began his life as Juan Rodríguez and gave himself the added name of "Cabrillo" much later, after he had

*Courtesy
Cabrillo National
Monument*

16

acquired property and social reputation. It might have started as a nickname or a link to a city of origin. But from a person who shied away from mention of his parents or upbringing, this conclusion is suspect. More likely, as "Juan Rodríguez" was a relatively common name in New Spain, Cabrillo's choice of a new surname stood as a method to distinguish a man of status from other Juan Rodríguez's, possibly of lower eminence.

There were many examples in Spain and Portugal of children taking names connected with their father, mother, relatives, or just friends. Historian Harry Kelsey concluded simply that, "surnames in the sixteenth century were as much a matter of choice as given names are now." What might have been surprising is that Cabrillo did not start using this surname until late in life. The first recorded use of the name Juan Rodríguez Cabrillo did not occur until July 1536, when *adelantado* Pedro de Alvarado rewarded Cabrillo by naming him *encomendero* in a formal document for the pueblos of Teota and Cotela.

For whatever reason Juan Rodríguez chose "Cabrillo," it was a choice of genius. In one swoop, Cabrillo improved his uniqueness and position. During both his time and through the records of history, a new, discrete, identifiable individual arose – one who could command the attention of those he led as well as generate a unique historical legacy.

As a trained crossbowman in a battalion led by

Pánfilo de Narváez, Cabrillo reached Mexico in 1520, and joined the forces of Hernán Cortés. The Spanish crossbow of the period was deadly accurate to fifty or seventy yards and represented one of several high-tech weapons available to conquistadors which the natives could not match.

Cabrillo served through some of Cortés' bloodiest battles of the Aztec campaign, including the attack on the Aztec capital, across the causeways of Lake Texcoco. He also showed nautical talent and boat skills for the first time, helping the Spanish army build boats for amphibious attacks. Following the defeat of the Aztecs, Cabrillo chose to accompany Pedro de Alvarado, Cortés' second-in-command, on the conquest of Guatemala. Capable and loyal, Cabrillo quickly rose to become Alvarado's trusted lieutenant.

In Guatemala, Cabrillo finally came into his own. He rose rapidly in local society both as a conquistador with an excellent military record and with high-level sponsors who were quick to reward his loyalty and faithful service. Importantly, Cabrillo advanced in life by taking calculated risks. His business, his colonial positions, and his family life were all intertwined. He stretched to invest in new ventures, some highly risky.

Not all of his endeavors and speculations proved successful, but he maintained a solid trajectory of success through his life while accumulating land, wealth, family, and standing, until he was recognized as a *hidalgo* in Spanish society. His business holdings were highly diversified: plantation farming, mining, shipping, shipbuilding, and it was not long before Cabrillo stood as one of the wealthiest noblemen of Guatemala.

Cabrillo's social standing depended, in large measure, on the *encomienda* system of New Spain. This social system, medieval in its roots, provided a chosen nobleman the personal services and tribute of those in selected villages. Under the *encomienda*, a nobleman had the right to demand goods, services or crops through annual fees. In exchange, the nobleman (or *encomendero*) supposedly provided governance, protection and religious guidance to the Native population.

Rights to *encomienda* villages came and went between noblemen, but it was clear that Cabrillo controlled quite a few. Cabrillo's use of *encomienda* labor provided the cornerstone of his wealth and business. Lucrative as they were, several Spanish noblemen brashly

"To his growing reputation as landowner, businessman and nobleman, one must also include Cabrillo's distinction as mariner and shipowner."

claimed Cabrillo *encomiendas* almost immediately after his death.

While exploiting native labor, Cabrillo swiftly expanded his holdings and profitable mining ventures to become one of the most significant landowners in Guatemala. Cabrillo returned to Seville to marry, travelling to Guatemala in 1533 with his bride. By 1536, his family had been blessed with the birth of two sons.

To his growing reputation as landowner, businessman and nobleman, one must also include Cabrillo's distinction as mariner and shipowner. Seafaring trade and shipbuilding were new industries in Guatemala during the 1520s and 1530s and Cabrillo's fame as a mariner raised his prestige and influence at the highest levels of government.

When the viceroy of New Spain formally applied his seal to the letter designating Cabrillo as the *captain-general* of the ambitious 1542 expedition to California, he selected the most trusted and respected person he could. This decision was not made lightly. Not only would this expedition be important for the future of New Spain, but much of the viceroy's personal fortune would ride on the voyage's success.

It was clear that Cabrillo stood prominently in the society of New Spain, unhindered by a lack of family lineage. His rise to the leadership of a crucial and conspicuous venture of the Crown was a reflection of personal ambition, business savvy, professional skills and excellent connections. Above all, Cabrillo possessed a gift of leadership mixed with perspective and inspirational skill. During an era when voyages of discovery were frequently dogged by mutinies, seamanship fiascos, political rivalries, weak leadership, distasteful interaction with indigenous peoples, or fainthearted pessimism; Cabrillo's strengths in each of these dimensions stood in sharp contrast.

By good fortune, careful advancement, and focused determination, the Juan Rodríguez Cabrillo of 1542, aboard the galleon *San Salvador*, was a fortuitous blend of warrior, baron, navigator, commander, seaman and shipwright. The successful return of *San Salvador* to Navidad – largely unscathed and with a bonanza of discoveries in her logs, charts, and holds – was in large part due to these personal strengths.

San Salvador ◆ Cabrillo's Galleon of Discovery

Chapter 2

The Building of the Galleon San Salvador

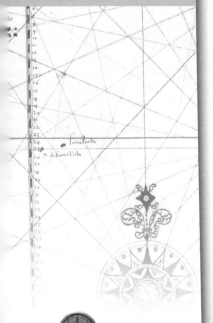

T he ship that had been venerated with the auspicious name *San Salvador* first emerged from the mud and shadows of a formless tropical forest in 1539. Here, at the far edge of the New World's frontier and in the damp hollows of sweltering coastal lowlands, sat a primitive shipyard of New Spain.

Although isolated and crude, in a region of New Spain that would later be called Guatemala, this shipyard represented the vanguard of Spanish ambitions along the Pacific coast. Active already for several years, by 1539 the shipyard bustled on a daily basis with an air of enthusiasm and progress. The yard stood as an essential centerpiece for a fleet of thirteen vessels, then under construction, to extend the imperial realm of the Spanish king and Holy Roman Emperor, Charles V, both northward along New Spain's west coast and westward across the Pacific.

Snaking through forested uplands and then across a wide coastal plain, the river Michatoya of Guatemala finally sought the ocean shore near the small fishing village of Iztapa. There, the river widened and slowed and turned parallel to the coastline, carving out a middling harbor behind a large bar of chalky white sand before finally spilling into the sea. The small shipyard, with its cluster of huts and clapboard storehouses, occupied a convenient, flat, muddy site just a half-league up-river at Gibaltique.

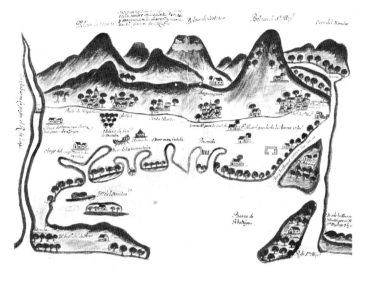

Along this stretch of lonely coast, floppy-leafed banana trees, jungle ferns and beach palms swayed to breezes heavy with humidity. Iztapa's tropical climate ensured warm and sticky conditions throughout the year as the damp air routinely collected in sodden clouds high over the interior or in the gray mists of jungle afternoons. Precipitation provided the sole definition for the seasons at Iztapa with a rainy season from May until October offsetting dry conditions for the balance of the year. Those who rose for work every morning at Iztapa were sure to remember the dampness, but they were just as likely to remember the incessant clatter from the nearby forests, the buzz and whir of insects mixing with the caws and jabber of a million birds.

The advantages for the shipbuilder were many at Iztapa. Lumber was plentiful in this tropical climate where towering trees and luxuriant creepers ascended from the riverbank. Large ocean-going ships could be drawn up and repaired on the marshy shores of the low-lying river. Fishing and farming

A hand-drawn sketch dating to the seventeenth century shows the Guatemalan coastline near Iztapa with the Michatoya River to the right and the location of the old Spanish shipyard at Gibaltique.
Courtesy Huntington Library

were productive, and the well-protected harbor provided the means to easily transport the building materials needed for ships. With few other protected bays along this sweep of coastline, Iztapa's simple harbor and fledgling shipyard drew many a Spaniard intent on exploration and ocean-going trade, as did the next fishing village, Acajutla, 65 miles further to the south.

As Spanish conquests expanded across Central America in the early sixteenth century, it soon became apparent that Spanish ships operating along Pacific coasts were essential for New Spain's success. Not only were ships needed to transport the riches of Peru to reach the treasure fleets returning to Spain, but only ships could explore the Spanish domains across the Pacific and protect them from the intruders of other nations.

Ships of the day were the most complex and most efficient mobile machines invented by man. A single ship, perhaps crewed by twenty-five men, could carry the cargo equivalent of fifty large wagons – wagons that would require a hundred coachmen and would be pulled by four-hundred horses. A ship would not need expensive networks of roads and would not be blocked by mountains, rivers, or national borders.

A ship, then as now, reflects immense complexity and a high degree

Note the construction sequence of *San Salvador* **as was probably followed in Guatemala in 1539-1540, beginning with the laying of the keel, then attaching frames, then continuing with decks, sides and hull.**

Courtesy Naval Architect
Doug Sharp, Sharp Design

of self-sufficiency in order to survive for months and years in a daunting hostile environment far from home. The strength of the Spanish global empire and its aspirations for exploration depended upon its ships – ships that could stand up to the demanding conditions of the high seas. Shipbuilders created designs every part of which stood for strength, flexibility, and reliability.

Important as ships were for Spain, it was impractical for Spanish ships in the Pacific to be supplied from European ports or shipyards. Sailing distances to the Pacific were great and any voyage around Cape Horn or through the Straits of Magellan ranked as arduous and risky. To solve this dilemma, conquistador Hernán Cortés strongly advocated building new vessels entirely along the west coast of New Spain. Cortés' first Pacific shipyard rose at Zacatula, near the mouth of the Balsas River, circa 1522, where three ships of Alvaro de Saavedra Cerón's Pacific expedition were built. Later, Cortés sponsored shipyard developments at Tehuantepec and Acapulco. Shipbuilding became the first major industrial activity of New Spain and in the New World administered by Europeans.

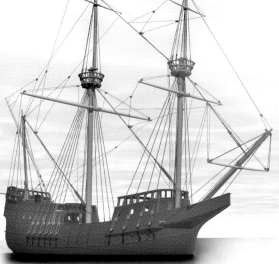

During the 1520s the Spanish army in Guatemala, with Juan Rodríguez Cabrillo assigned as a captain of crossbowmen, conquered vast swaths of land and established a

San Salvador ◆ *Cabrillo's Galleon of Discovery*

provincial capital and army garrison at the town of Santiago about fifteen leagues inland from the Pacific shore. By the early 1530s, Cortés' shipbuilding initiatives had spread to Guatemala encouraged mainly by the demands of Peruvian trade. All this activity was certain to have caught the attention of Cabrillo, who was growing in influence with an expanding fortune and a thriving estate in Santiago.

There is some evidence that Cabrillo had long had an interest in shipbuilding that may have predated his arrival in the New World. In 1521, Cabrillo assisted with the building of thirteen oar-powered *bergantines* used in Cortés' final amphibious assault across the Aztec causeways in Mexico City. It was said by his peers that Cabrillo assisted with these vessels because "he was a man of the sea and understood it all." Attracted by the generous profits in trade with Peru (with horses, army supplies, and colonial needs flowing to Peru and treasure flowing in return), Cabrillo built a trading galleon named *Santiago* in Acajutla by 1533. Although not successful in this venture, Cabrillo gained useful experience in west coast shipbuilding and earned valuable recognition throughout the Spanish community as an able mariner.

Several historians have noted that the first generation of Pacific coast ships sponsored by Cortés were of poor quality with craftsmanship suffering from inexperience and inferior materials. By the late 1530s, though, green Guatemalan craftsmen had been trained, supply efforts streamlined, and shipbuilding processes honed.

At this same time, the *adelantado* (military governor) of Guatemala, Don Pedro de Alvarado, set out to organize a new fleet of vessels for expeditions of discovery into the Pacific, efforts sanctioned by a special royal charter awarded by the Spanish crown. Alvarado named Cabrillo *justicia mayor* (chief magistrate) at the port of Iztapa and his primary shipwright to oversee the fleet's organization and construction.

Alvarado's wish was for thirteen vessels. Some were older first-generation ships that would be hauled out of the water, replanked, and refurbished. To round out the rest of the fleet, Cabrillo constructed seven or eight other vessels between 1536 and 1540. Others were invited to join this venture by supplying their own ships or sponsoring those under construction with the promise to ultimately share in any expedition profits. It was in this vein that *San Salvador* became a reality. With Cabrillo already engaged in the construction and refitting of the Alvarado fleet, it was a natural step to supply his own funds for the building of one of the fleet's ships – a sturdy merchant galleon to be built to his own design.

As famous as *San Salvador* grew to be, no plans for her design have survived the years since the sixteenth century. Neither hull dimensions nor images of the ship exist and no record of her demise, or evidence of shipwreck, have been found. What is known through historical research is that Gonzalo Fernández de Oviedo, the first official chronicler of the Spanish Indies, described Alvarado's armada as three galleons of more than 200 *toneladas*, an oar-powered galley, two *fustas*

A depiction of *San Salvador* **under full sail by artist Richard DeRosset, who represents well the relative size of crewmembers to ship.**
MMSD Collections

27

> **"He charged me with building an armada [of thirteen ships] for him..."**
>
> – Juan Rodríguez Cabrillo

(light vessels with one or two masts and oars), and several lighter vessels. Eight of these ships were newly built and Alvarado specified that they be raised at the port of Iztapa. Oviedo also wrote of a painting (now long lost) of the fleet that had been prepared for the Spanish court to commemorate this exciting milestone in the history of New Spain.

The first official mention of the ship *San Salvador* appeared in a 1541 legal deposition by Juan Rodríguez Cabrillo, documenting the debts owed him, her owner, after the death of *adelantado* Alvarado. "He charged me with building an armada [of thirteen ships] for him," Cabrillo testified, "and I built it and served in the said armada which is the one he brought to this port of la Navidad and with my own means I built a ship named Sant Salvador [sic] which is anchored in this port and at my expense without the governor or his stewards putting anything whatever into it." Together, these published records provided the first clues of *San Salvador's* dimensions – a galleon of more than 200 *toneladas*.

Spanish shipbuilders routinely followed guidelines and regulations, approved by the Crown, defining a ship's size. The Spanish use of the *tonelada* measurement in the mid-sixteenth century was a measure of capacity or volume, roughly equivalent to "tonnage" in

modern vernacular. Historian Carla Rahn
illips has explained that a *tonelada* involves
ear measures in *codos* derived from a
mula equaling (Depth) times (½ Beam) times
ngth). Although this definition involves
eral variables, her study of the recorded
mensions of several other Spanish ships
the era provides a good appreciation of
n Salvador's scope that can now be
imated. From the tip of her beakhead to
taffrail, *San Salvador* would have measured
ne 90 feet in length and 25 feet in beam,
th a size of about 90 tons in modern units.

he design of a sixteenth-century Spanish
galleon evolved from that of the *carrack*
nao of the late fifteenth century. Typically,
alleon's forecastle stood much lower than
aftercastle, giving the ship a distinctive
v-slung crescent-shape, quite different
m most other European ships. This
ercastle at the stern was particularly
tinctive in galleons with a sharp square
d that stood high out of the water.
ditionally, Spanish galleons sported two
ly-planked decks suitable for cargo and
rage, a half-deck aft of the mainmast, a
aracteristic decorated beakhead below the
wsprit (harkening back to the "ramming
k" of Mediterranean war galleys), and the
lity to carry armament.

Adze

Broad-axe

Jungle machete

Auger

The adze, broad-axe,
jungle machete and
auger were all common
shipyard tools in
Guatemala and New
Spain. The adze was
particularly effective for
shipbuilders for finely
shaping wooden hulls.
Larger augers sometimes
required two men to
twist them for drilling
into wood.

Galleons were usually ship-rigged with three masts – the forward two masts each held two square sails and the mizzenmast held a triangular lateen sail. They represented a marriage of Atlantic and Mediterranean shipbuilding techniques that had steadily improved through the ages. Although some European galleons featured a fourth mast, called a Bonaventure-mizzen aft of the mizzen, indirect records from *San Salvador's* voyage indicate she was ship-rigged with three masts. Additionally, *San Salvador* included a small spritsail on the bowsprit to help in maneuvering. With this three-masted combination of square and lateen sails and a sternpost rudder, the full-rigged ship of the sixteenth century was a balanced and maneuverable vessel, tough enough to withstand the rigors of open sea.

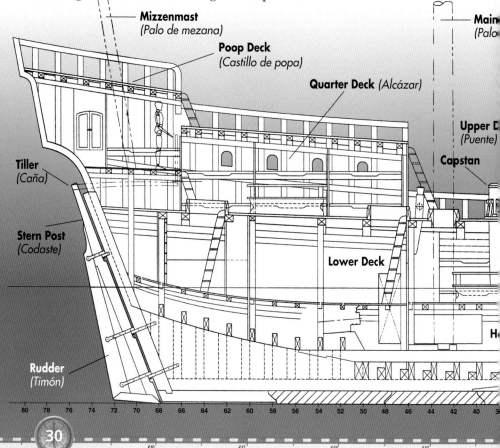

Mizzenmast
(Palo de mezana)

Main
(Palo

Poop Deck
(Castillo de popa)

Quarter Deck (Alcázar)

Upper D
(Puente)

Tiller
(Caña)

Capstan

Stern Post
(Codaste)

Lower Deck

Rudder
(Timón)

H

80 78 76 74 72 70 68 66 64 62 60 58 56 54 52 50 48 46 44 42 40 3

For its time, the Spanish galleon was a successful, durable and powerful concept and its features found their way into the ship designs of Portugal, Holland and England. The galleon era spanned 250 years and included many examples of galleons in pure freight-carrying configurations, some as combined cargo and passenger vessels, and some as warships. In Cabrillo's time, galleon designs favored cargo-carrying, and most historians have described *San Salvador* as a "merchant galleon".

It cannot be forgotten that *San Salvador's* ultimate design reflected the simplicity of New Spain's construction realities, built far from the established shipyards of Europe.

This cut-away architectural drawing shows the interior detail of *San Salvador*. The crew lived, worked and ate on the main deck. The two levels below the main deck were for stores, cargo, animals, and (in the lowest possible position) stone and sand ballast.

Courtesy Naval Architect Doug Sharp, Sharp Design

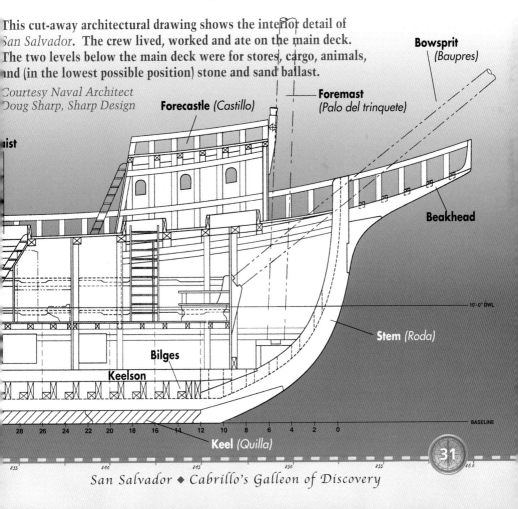

Bowsprit (Baupres)

Forecastle (Castillo)

Foremast (Palo del trinquete)

Beakhead

aist

10'-0" DWL

Stem (Roda)

Bilges

Keelson

28 26 24 22 20 18 16 14 12 10 8 6 4 2 0

Keel (Quilla)

BASELINE

31

235 240 245 250 255 260

San Salvador ◆ *Cabrillo's Galleon of Discovery*

Engraving by Flemish painter Pieter Bruegel, the Elder, showing the flexibility of the basic galleon design of the mid-sixteenth century. This armed galleon is sailing from a European port and features about 22 guns, as well as a fourth mast called a Bonaventure-mizzen. Both mizzen masts carry lateen sails. Lateen sails were originally popular in the Mediterranean and the northern Indian Ocean and were introduced into Northern European ship designs in combination with square sails to provide better maneuverability and steering while improving sailing ability upwind.

Here, materials differed from those of Spain, and designers, shipwrights, and craftsmen largely lacked European experience and building processes were less ordered.

Ships of the era (including those of the distant Pacific coast) were not constructed from rigid plans laid down on paper. Although the Spanish crown regularly approved standards for different types and configurations of ships, these standards were merely "rules of thumb" in practical use. Original concepts and first plans for Pacific ships rarely survived the builder's initial crisis, whether caused by supplies, workmanship, or technique. The flexibility

of Pacific shipwrights was constantly tested through trimming, adjusting, and shaping during every week of the building phase. No two ships ever looked exactly alike, and there are stories in the historical record of the final product looking dramatically dissimilar from the initial vision.

Ships of any era carry a staggering variety of technologies that span an immense scope, all carefully centralized within the tight confines of a single location. For *San Salvador*, hundreds of pulleys, a labyrinth of fixed and running rigging, and cannons of wrought iron shared the same space with a rugged capstan to lift the heaviest of objects, and precision instruments that could

Carpentry was a labor intensive and demanding part of shipbuilding in the sixteenth century. Carpenters in large numbers were required to form and fit the thousands of wood items needed for ships of the era.
MMSD Collections

A great quantity of rope and line was required for sixteenth century sailing ships and those ships built in New Spain primarily used native pita, sisal and hemp fibers from plants such as agave succulents. These tough fibers would be rendered from plants and then hand strung or twisted into threads, strands, lines, and cables.

measure the tiniest variations in the movements of celestial objects high in the sky.

The shipwrights, chief constructors, and craftsmen of Iztapa learned their trade in the midst of revolutionary advances in European ship design during the sixteenth century. These advances included the combined use of square sails and triangular lateen sails, the design of a high aftercastle, wide beams and pronounced tumblehome sides for stability, and the building process of erecting skeletal ribs covered by planking. Pacific coast shipwrights were attentive to European advances and fully integrated them into their own designs. Despite this, ship constructors in New Spain were conservative, careful and plodding for there was little opportunity to recover from mistakes.

The Iztapa labor force came largely from Indian *cuadrillas*, effectively slave labor organized and directed by native foremen. The raw industrial operations of the shipyard involved hundreds, perhaps thousands, of Indian workers, similar to the practice of Spanish mines in the New World. Slaving expeditions across the countryside were not uncommon, including natives who collected other natives from different tribes in return for a Spanish bounty.

Indian work parties were routinely pressed into service to provide timber and the raw materials for shipbuilding. They carried these materials over great distances and along primitive trails at, undoubtedly, a great toll among the native conscripts. Others farmed and fished to provide subsistence for those at the shipyard, while some Indians who showed talent were elevated to overseer or apprenticeship roles. Africans also worked in Pacific shipyards and were allocated to ships.

Timber, as well as the pita fiber needed for a vessel's cables and rigging, was plentiful near the river Michatoya. Other maritime supplies such as pitch, tar, resins, and oils were also sought locally. Selection of the varieties and quality of wood was crucial, and the master builder probably accompanied the logging parties to ensure the best selections. The most difficult timbers to find were those tall and straight for masts and spars. They were carefully culled from the vast supplies and kept at a separate location on the grounds of the shipyard.

With shipbuilding in process, a lasting haze lay across Iztapa and filtered the light throughout

Simple forges were in continuous use in the shipyards of New Spain supplementing ironwork imported from Europe. Such items as common nails and bolts, iron fittings for the rudder, anchor stock or longboat, strengtheners for the mast, and various deck fittings all required metal work performed by skilled blacksmiths. Shown is Blacksmith Theodore Scott, of San Diego, reenacting the art of metalwork at the building site of the replica *San Salvador*.

San Salvador ◆ Cabrillo's Galleon of Discovery

the forest. This smoke rose from simple blacksmith forges and tallow braziers, and was spiced with pungent whiffs of kindling and hot pitch. Although most of a ship's complex ironwork came from European shipments, Spanish blacksmiths created nails and basic iron pieces directly at the Iztapa forge. Other shipbuilding materials were likewise imported from Europe when they could not be easily manufactured locally. When Alvarado returned from a trip to Spain in 1539, for instance, he brought with him large supplies of sails, rigging, ironwork, anchors, artillery and other materials for his fleet.

As her owner was also her builder, *San Salvador* enjoyed a distinctive advantage among the ships at Iztapa. Cabrillo constantly oversaw each of the many decisions of her final shape and, undoubtedly, carefully saved the finest materials and assigned the most talented tradesmen to her construction. Likewise, Cabrillo's foremen

Construction of the replica *San Salvador,* **at Spanish Landing in San Diego, shows the first U-shaped frame and its attachment to the keel.**

Courtesy Tony Enyedy

certainly stayed alert to the owner's attention and applied that little bit of extra effort to achieve Cabrillo's appreciation. It is quite reasonable to assume that *San Salvador* reached an unusually high level of perfection for a ship built in the Guatemalan wilderness.

San Salvador's construction began with the building of its keel, or *quilla* in Spanish. Blocks were first placed in the muddy building-way immediately next to the river's damp shore, and stout local timbers were then joined together atop them to form the keel. To this basic piece of the ship's structural spine, the shipwright then attached the curved stempost, called the *roda*. Matching this at the keel's aft end, workers attached a straight sternpost (*codaste* in Spanish) and braced it to lean backward in the air.

With these first steps construction shifted to the ribs of the ship and the principal essence of the ship began to take shape. Each frame for the ship's ribs contained several different pieces painstakingly cut in the sawpits and joined into large "U" shapes by carpenters and sawyers. These were attached perpendicular to the keel, frame-by-frame, to prepare the ship's skeleton – an exacting step. Each frame stood unique from every other one, and the rhythmic swoosh of saws and the raw thuds from the adze told different stories as each frame emerged.

The first frames joined to the keel were the largest and were placed about one-third of the distance from stem to stern. As frames were added aft toward the sternpost, their shapes became more of a "Y" than a "U" with the bottom of each "Y" attached to the keel. The breadth of each frame narrowed as it progressed toward the stern.

The complex curves of the finished hull represented both a challenge and an art form to the shipbuilder. Designed properly, the ship would gracefully slide through water; designed poorly, with mistakes in framing, the ship would be doomed to a cumbersome and plodding life. To set the curve of the hull, *San Salvador's* builder

A model of *San Salvador*, by master ship modeler Joe Bompensiero, shows a representation of how the frames for the ship are designed and built to add strength, flexibility and durability to the ship's entire structure, allowing the ship to survive in high seas.

Photos by Ted Walton

attached a series of narrow strips of wood, called the wales, to the top of the skeleton. By sharpness of eye, or simply by the feel of running a hand down a hull, the builder adjusted the wales to smooth the curve of the ship from bow to stern. Once the basic ribs were in place, others were added for strength, until a giant skeleton was in place formed by about thirty different frames.

Planks for *San Salvador's* hull came from supple softwoods found in the nearby wilderness. Cut thick and sturdy, these boards were steamed in long planking boxes. Once the planks became soft and pliable they were rushed to the framed-up hull where

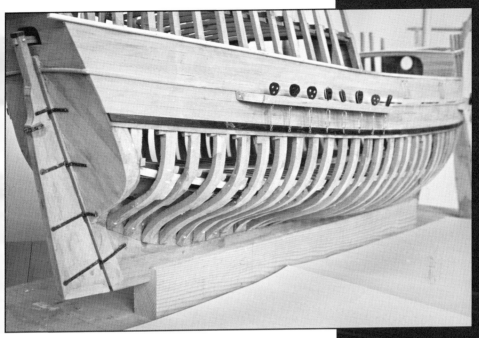

they were wedged and clamped into place, then fastened by iron spikes or wooden pins.

As a final step, all seams between the hull planks were caulked with pieces of tarred hemp applied with a caulking mallet. Then, the entire structure was coated in tallow and pitch. Although all ships of this era were coated in grease, several surviving documents specifically refer to *San Salvador* as the "black galleon". This is a clue that *San Salvador* stood out even blacker than others, probably indicating excellent watertightness.

In European practice the hull was further protected from shipworms by nailing a piece of tarred cloth to the underwater hull and then covering that with a thin sheathing of lead. Chances are that this did not occur with Guatemalan-built ships, but there is evidence

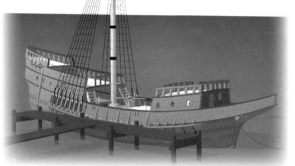

that Spanish Pacific ships were often anchored in fresh river water to avoid teredo (shipworms) attack, or were periodically drawn from the water to lie on a beach for repair from their damage.

Courtesy Naval Architect Doug Sharp, Sharp Design

It is not certain how *San Salvador* was first introduced to the muddy Michatoya, whether by a stern-first launch down an inclined building-way or by slowly flooding a primitive "drydock" manually dug behind

To step the mast and rig the ship, a pair of large wooden spars or tree trunks called "sheers" were positioned on deck to act as a crane. A line was run from the top of the sheers to near the middle balance point of the mast. The mast was then carefully lifted and hauled to a near-vertical position and guided into a hole in the deck and lowered onto the "step" – a large block of wood on the ship's keelson. The mast was secured in a vertical position with the use of tensioned standing rigging. The mainmast was raised first, followed by the foremast and mizzen. Once the lower masts were in place, top masts were added to the main and foremasts, yards were raised by halyards to hold the sails, and then the final rigging put in place.

the river's edge. Regardless, the event was one of great anxiety as there was no foolproof way in advance of the launch to ensure categorically that the thousand elements of a ship's design would merge into a vessel that could actually float. Everyone viewing the launch had heard tales of, or actually witnessed, ships capsizing at launch or springing an uncontrollable

leak when her seams and water integrity were first tested. Faced with this uncertainty and risk, priests were present, prayers were rendered, and owner Juan Rodríguez was probably holding his breath.

From all accounts, the launch went well and *San Salvador* was next ballasted with heavy stones in her hold. Her masts were brought to the ship to be stepped, while she was lashed to simple piles in the river. The tall spires were carefully prepared in advance in the shipyard: first hewn and tapered by skilled woodsmen, then squared, then made eight-sided, then sixteen-sided and finally round. Heavy masts and yardarms were hoisted and swayed into place by the use of simple block-and-tackle shears. Once braced in place, standing rigging (greased hemp cordage) was

fixed in position and tensioned to support the masts. Running rigging was added to handle the operation of the sails and yards.

Thousands of maritime accoutrements were assembled for *San Salvador* during its final months of fitting out including anchors, capstans, pumps, brass and iron fittings, and the rudder. Carpenters and apprentices fanned out around the ship on a hundred tasks as their skills turned to companion ways, hatch covers, paneling, ladders, scuttles, and carefully carved decorative work. A ceremonial picture, probably with a religious theme befitting the ship's name, might have been painted across the transom. *San Salvador* carried a small collection of cannon, perhaps four to six (normally stowed below decks), and the ship's design included a small powder magazine space below decks.

Once ready for sea, many referred to the ship as *Juan Rodríguez*, as Spanish ships commonly held the name of their owners. Cabrillo took his new pride-and-joy on a trading voyage to Peru, hoping to offset some of her construction costs (estimated to be some 4000 castellanos de oro de minas, not an insignificant sum) through trade profits. The voyage provided the opportunity to test the ship and adjust her sailing qualities.

During her trials, every element of *San Salvador's* operation was tested – from the performance of her rudder and capstan to that of her guns. Trim and ballast adjustments occurred after testing in different conditions of wind and seas. Her caulking and seams were continuously inspected, as were the operation of pumps. Sails were lofted in different combinations and deficiencies corrected. Above all, Cabrillo focused on the detailed training of his crew to prepare them for longer voyages. Drills, practice and exercises were probably a daily occurrence – all conducted under the captain's (and owner's) careful observation. Strong, experienced crew were unquestionably identified and encouraged; weaker sailors were weeded out.

By the time *San Salvador* returned to Guatemala, Cabrillo had a

veteran ship, thoroughly tested and finely tuned. Time was short to prepare the ship for her next voyage and Cabrillo's activity was undoubtedly focused on lists of repairs and modifications, and he was scouring Spanish port towns for any replacement crew or new seagoing specialists.

San Salvador represented a powerful implement of Spanish influence and strength. The combination of a heavy frame-built design, a proven and complex sailing rig, a sternpost rudder for superb control, and powerful artillery, all worked together to create or exceed any threat of the day: Native, Asiatic, or European. By the time the tropical rainy season of 1542 had begun, San Salvador stood fully prepared and ready for the next challenge that was sure to come her way.

A computer rendering of how San Salvador **might have looked under sail.**

Courtesy Digital Navy

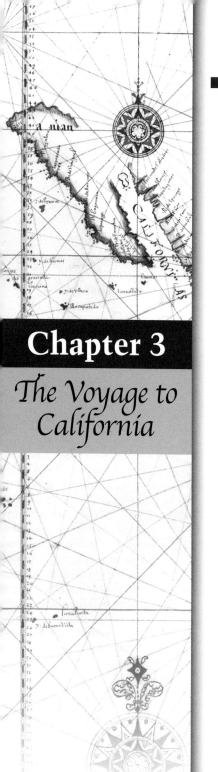

Chapter 3

The Voyage to California

*T*he twenty years immediately preceding *San Salvador's* epic quest of California were years of bold discovery along the Pacific Ocean coast of New Spain. Following the Spanish conquest of the Aztec Empire, Spanish conquistador Hernán Cortés moved to solidify Spanish rule throughout central New Spain beginning in 1522, and established a series of small ports that looked out toward the western sunset. Once on the shore of the great South Sea, Spanish goals were twofold: first, to pursue Columbus' original dream of trade with the Orient and, second, to explore north and south along the coast hoping to find greater riches and extend the reach of Spanish settlements.

While others reached for wealth to the south along the Pacific coast, Cortés sought royal sponsors for ventures northward. Reports of gold and pearls to the north stirred his excitement as well as, perhaps, the discovery of the rumored island of "California" populated by Amazon women. One of Cortés' priorities might also have included finding the long-sought Northwest Passage linking the Atlantic and Pacific and its western terminus, referred to later as the Strait of Anián. It was an article of faith that an oceanic passage, similar to the Straits of

Magellan, existed far to the north of the American landmass, as land certainly would not extend as far as the North Pole. Not only could Anián serve as a shortcut to and from Europe, benefiting Spanish settlement, but fortifying the Strait could also block the ships of others from challenging Spanish claims in the Pacific. Finding this Strait would polish the reputation of any discoverer to a great luster, it would guarantee his standing at the Spanish court, and, perhaps, would even win a royal prize.

Most felt that Cortés was correct in seeking his fortune to the north. An abundance of gold and silver had already been won from the Aztecs, and Francisco Pizarro had pried great treasures from the Incas by the early 1530s. It appeared reasonable to assume that a similarly rich nation could lie just beyond the northern horizon. Every conquistador of New Spain hoped to find his own Peru, and northward was the direction least explored.

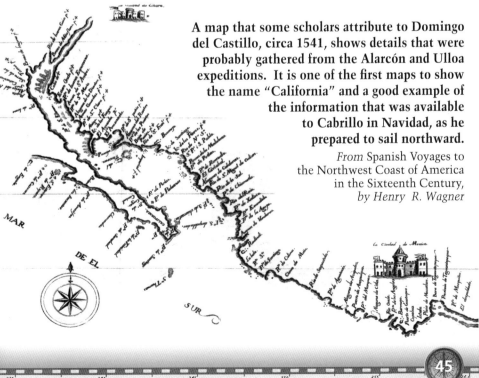

A map that some scholars attribute to Domingo del Castillo, circa 1541, shows details that were probably gathered from the Alarcón and Ulloa expeditions. It is one of the first maps to show the name "California" and a good example of the information that was available to Cabrillo in Navidad, as he prepared to sail northward.

From Spanish Voyages to the Northwest Coast of America in the Sixteenth Century, *by Henry R. Wagner*

In 1532, 1533 and 1535, Cortés sponsored three ventures northward up the west coast of New Spain. Sailing in seas never before seen by Europeans and 150 miles from the mainland, the Spaniards spied the prominent southern tip of a large new land – apparently an island and possibly California. Personally leading the third of these expeditions, Cortés reached Baja California with three vessels, but an ill-fated settlement at La Paz did not last for want of supplies.

Still fascinated by prospects to the north, Cortés sponsored an expedition commanded by the energetic Francisco de Ulloa that sailed from Acapulco in 1539. This voyage of discovery touched at La Paz and then re-crossed the gulf to sail farther along the New Spain mainland to the bay of Guaymas. Seeking the northern end of the "island" of California, Ulloa, instead, discovered violent tides and discolored water from the outwash of the Colorado River. This was the first indication that Baja California was not an island at all, but a lengthy peninsula separated from New Spain by the narrow Gulf of California. Ulloa came about, sailed southward, and rounded Cabo San Lucas at the tip of Baja California. He then journeyed along the western Baja California coast as far north as Isla de Cedros. There, one ship returned home while the flagship continued northward for another two hundred miles before finally returning to New Spain by the summer of 1540.

While Ulloa's voyage was still in progress, the newly named Viceroy of New Spain, Antonio de Mendoza, pressed his own designs northward with a two-pronged land and sea expedition to find the fabled Seven Cities of Gold. Beginning in February 1540, the able Francisco Vásquez de Coronado led the land procession northward, while the sea detachment, commanded by Hernando de Alarcón, followed three months later. Alarcón confirmed Ulloa's discoveries and then explored the Colorado River to a point just south of present-day Yuma.

Spanish Advances
Northward Along the
Pacific Coast of New Spain
1535 -1542

oining the growing chorus of conquistadors looking northward, the powerful military governor of Guatemala, Pedro de Alvarado, obtained his own royal charter to explore both to the north and to the west across the Pacific. Promising a fleet of over a dozen vessels to accomplish new exploration, Alvarado entered into a shrewd arrangement with Viceroy Mendoza to share expedition expenses and rewards. Alvarado's fleet

San Salvador ◆ Cabrillo's Galleon of Discovery

Inside map (as legible labels): Cathay, Quinfay, Archipelagus 7448 Infularũ, Chamaho, Temiftitan, Panico Inf. Tornacarũ, Terra florida, FRANCISCA, C. Brenon, Exterior, Oceanus occidentalis, CVBA, Iamica, Dominica, S. Iacobi, Amile, Inf. Hefperidum, Medera, Fortunatæ Inf., M. pdomum, PARIA, Die Nüw Infulñ At Dieles quam uocant Brafilli & Americam, Canibale, Hatigara, Inf. infortunatæ, Calenfuan, Welt, Regio Gigantum, 7. inf. ile Mar querirarũ, Mare pacificum, Fretum Magalani

German cosmographer Sebastian Munster drew this map, circa 1540, and printed it by wood block for wide distribution. It represents the perception of the geography of the Americas during the period that Cabrillo sailed, including the belief that northern America stretched toward Asia and that the Pacific was relatively small in breadth, with the islands of Japan near to the California coast.

MMSD Map and Chart Collections

would be the largest yet assembled along the Spanish west coast. To handle the intricate plans for organizing his ships, Alvarado turned to his long-trusted lieutenant, Juan Rodríguez Cabrillo. One of Cabrillo's first assignments was to establish a new port, big enough for the anticipated armada and one that Alvarado could control. Cabrillo scouted to the north of Guatemala and discovered a promising harbor location at a site to be named Navidad.

Everyone sensed the growing momentum for adventure that hung around Alvarado's activities. By December 1540, Alvarado's design focused on two simultaneous expeditions, one westward toward the Orient and one northward along the coast of New Spain. Alvarado gathered his fleet at the west coast ports of Iztapa and Acajutla and then ordered Cabrillo to take the armada up to the new port of Navidad for final expedition preparations.

Native uprisings now took their toll on

Abrahamus Ortelius' 1589 map shows the common belief, which underpinned the Cabrillo expedition, that the Pacific was much smaller than its actual expanse and that by following the Pacific coastline of North America, supposedly curving toward the west, *San Salvador* could reach China, Japan, the Philippines, and the Spice Islands.

MMSD Map and Chart Collections

Alvarado's best-laid plans. Alvarado left his fleet under Cabrillo's care in early 1541 and headed to the interior to put down a major Indian uprising. Alvarado met a sudden end when his horse lost its footing during an engagement and crushed him to death. Viceroy Mendoza immediately claimed ownership of the ships owned by Alvarado, while others in the fleet drifted away. Cabrillo returned to Guatemala, probably taking *San Salvador* with him. Further throwing local Spanish rule into disarray, a natural disaster destroyed the Guatemalan government town of Santiago where Cabrillo had built his estate.

Despite the mounting calamities, plans for the twin explorations into the Pacific now realigned under the direction of Viceroy Mendoza. Well respected by both Alvarado and Mendoza, Cabrillo received a summons from the viceroy to return to Navidad in the spring of 1542. Sailing *San Salvador* to Navidad, Cabrillo again took charge of preparations for both expeditions to meet Mendoza's urgent new plans.

The viceroy's cousin, Ruy López de Villalobos, assumed command of six ships of the fleet to sail westward across the South Sea to reach the Spice Islands, while Cabrillo rose to *captain-general* of the northward venture. Mendoza assigned two ships to the northward expedition: Cabrillo's own *San Salvador* and a smaller cargo vessel of about 60-feet in length, *La Victoria*. In addition, the expedition included a small 30-foot *bergantín* or *fragata* named *San Miguel* that served as a tender for *San Salvador*, extending the flagship's capabilities. *San Miguel* had been designed for about a dozen pairs of oars and a sail and may have been covered partially by a deck to allow open ocean operation. With its light construction and shallow draught, *San Miguel* excelled at exploring inshore bays and estuaries. At times, the flagship towed the tiny *bergantín,* at other times she sailed independently.

These two voyages of discovery had different tactical objectives, but were closely intertwined both in their origin and anticipated destination. During the early sixteenth century most believed that the California coast bent westward as one sailed north, and maps of the period showed China and Japan just a short distance from the North American coast. If this reasoning held and if Cabrillo followed the California coast to the north, he would eventually reach the Orient after a long curving transit. If Villalobos sailed directly across the Pacific to reach the Indies, the explorers would meet, claim new domains, find a way back to New Spain, and enrich the viceroy. Cabrillo was to look for riches along the way, but his primary goal was to reach the Orient.

As well-deserved as it might have been, Cabrillo's appointment to *captain-general* of the northward expedition was an immense stroke of personal good fortune. By owning his own ship and as leader of the expedition, Cabrillo expected to earn a sizeable slice of any profits, especially lucrative if native gold or a route to China were discovered. Likewise, success in life and business within Spanish society was immensely influenced by patronage and Cabrillo's two principal sponsors, Cortés and Alvarado, could no longer help him in 1542. Without this thin thread of support extended by Viceroy Mendoza, Cabrillo's complex personal empire might well have crumbled.

Cabrillo now became busier then ever as Navidad hummed with activity and the ships made ready for their endeavors. The port of Navidad commanded a picturesque expanse of coastline, where several prominent headlands defined a series of scalloped bays with wide sandy beaches. At the southern end of these bays, where the forest reached down to the water, lay a broad half-moon inlet. Here, on a narrow spit of sand that separated the bay from a large lagoon fed by a lazy river that reached far away to the interior, Cabrillo had established his port.

Cabrillo had found this bay at the direction of Alvarado and Mendoza, who first visited the site on Christmas Day, 1540, and provided the harbor with a name to commemorate that event. In quick order, Navidad became a thriving maritime nexus for expeditions of discovery with a modest shipyard and supply center. The fresh water from the river provided protection from shipworms, and the low-lying mud and sandy shoreline of the lagoon offered a convenient location to draw ships from the water for hull repairs. In September 1541, two expeditions of discovery had sailed from Navidad: Hernando de Alarcón sailing on a return mission up the Gulf of California and Francisco de Bolaños sailing up the west coast of Baja California (where he foundered and became marooned).

By early 1542, vessels of every description crowded the Navidad lagoon while preparing for sea. Soldiers, sailors and laborers were everywhere. Smoke from construction fires and the sound of mallet, axe, and adze filled the air. Stories, logs and updates of nautical charts were the common fare among pilots and captains, and the latest information from plucky voyages was studiously copied into personal diaries or logs, referred to as "rutters". Cartography information was usually closely guarded as a state secret, but given the common community of pilots in Navidad and the royal sanction for *San Salvador's* voyage, Cabrillo was sure to have access to information from prior expeditions.

Fitting out the expedition ships for sea and accumulating the necessary stores and foodstuffs was an expensive proposition for the viceroy and ships' owners. Thousands of individual articles had to be purchased in advance, carefully dispatched, and then staged in crowded warehouses. Marine stores, biscuit barrels, cannon shot and water casks were mixed with livestock, personal chests, and spare cordage – all systematically organized and astutely assigned to individual ships.

There is some question as to whether Cabrillo or Villalobos departed first from Navidad, but both outfitted their ships during the spring and summer of 1542. The great prize for Villalobos was to challenge the

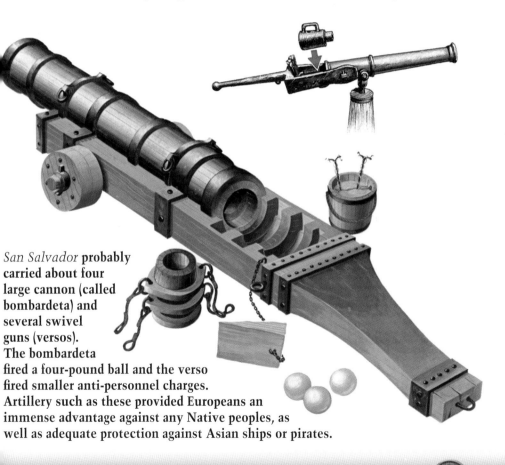

San Salvador **probably carried about four large cannon (called bombardeta) and several swivel guns (versos). The bombardeta fired a four-pound ball and the verso fired smaller anti-personnel charges. Artillery such as these provided Europeans an immense advantage against any Native peoples, as well as adequate protection against Asian ships or pirates.**

Portuguese monopoly in spices and develop a Spanish base in the Indies. Everyone knew that spices in Europe could command a hundred times their purchase price, a value rivaling that of gold or silver for traders.

Underway from Navidad, Villalobos sailed westward with six ships. He made rapid progress and sighted the islands of Eniwetok and Ulithi (in the mid-Pacific Caroline Islands), before finally reaching Mindanao in the Philippines. Challenged by the Portuguese, Villalobos tried to sail back to Mexico, but he could find no winds favorable for that west-to-east return voyage. Ultimately, Villalobos died of tropical fever in a Portuguese prison, but many members of his expedition eventually returned to Europe by Portuguese ships sailing across the Indian Ocean. On June 27, 1542, Viceroy Mendoza's northward expedition also set sail from Navidad. All hands were sent to weigh anchor and *San Salvador* made for the harbor's entrance with *Victoria* and *San Miguel* following. Ships of the sixteenth century routinely flew banners and ensigns of their owners or religious patrons. At least one reference indicates that Cabrillo flew the banner of a *captain-general* from *San Salvador's* foretopmast, indicating its status as flagship. The flag of the cross of Burgundy, the Spanish naval ensign, flew at the main truck, and Cabrillo probably ordered the flying of a personal banner as well. The ships hugged the familiar coastline in kind weather and with a fair wind astern. *Victoria* quickly took station as the flagship, with experienced navigator Bartolomé Ferrer acting as both her captain and the chief pilot for the overall expedition.

San Salvador set her course toward the cliffs of Cabo de Corrientes that soon loomed on the starboard bow forty leagues north of Navidad. The cape stood as a conspicuous landmark accurately plotted on the charts and *San Salvador* fixed her position before setting out into open sea. *San Salvador's* projected course took her directly to the tip of the California peninsula, which was sighted from the masthead on July 3, 1542. It was a solid, business-like beginning to the expedition, certainly establishing the *captain-general's* reputation as a careful and experienced sea captain. The conservative Cabrillo anchored for two days on the eastern shore of the tip of Baja California (which he referred to as *Punta de la California*), before sailing for a day to Cabo San Lucas to top-off water casks.

T he change in landscape during this first week of sailing was dramatic and sudden, shifting from the lush tropical scenery of Navidad to the bleak and desert-like surroundings of southern Baja California.

Sparse vegetation met everyone's landward gaze, while parched ridgelines stood in bold relief. Barren and deserted, as it surely appeared to the Spaniards, the shoreline teemed with life: sheerwaters swooping in the breeze, brown pelicans sailing in elongated formations

Illustration of San Salvador by Bruce Dragoo.

"I tell you, that on the right-hand side of the Indies there was an island called California, which was very close to the region of Earthly Paradise."

down the surfline, seals and sea lions sunning on the beaches. Temperatures in July were in the mid-90s during the day and mid-70s in the evenings and occasional showers were always expected. Most of the annual rainfall near Cabo San Lucas occurred in late summer from humid tropical flows or storms generated during the Baja California hurricane season.

The name "California" was already well in use by 1542. Most likely, the name was linked to the fictitious island from Garci Rodríguez de Montalvo's 1508 novel *Las Sergas de Esplandián*, where the beautiful Queen Calafia ruled over the Island of California and its population of attractive Amazon women.

"I tell you," de Montalvo's wrote, "that on the right-hand side of the Indies there was an island called California, which was very close to the region of Earthly Paradise. This island was inhabited by black women, and there were no males among them at all, for their life style was similar to that of the Amazons. The island was made up of the wildest cliffs and the sharpest precipices found anywhere in the world …." The name subsequently appeared in descriptions from the Ulloa expedition and on a map made by Domingo del Castillo in 1541.

S ome historians believe the name began as a bit of a joke, sarcastically comparing the bone-dry and destitute landscape of southern Baja California to the "earthly paradise" so well described in fiction. Whatever its specific source, "California" came into regular use by Spanish pilots and Cabrillo thought little of its use when he logged his arrival at *Punta de la California.*

After departing Cabo San Lucas, *San Salvador* bore off to the north making good, steady progress. An easy heaving under foot, the agreeable creaking of timbers, and rustle of sails in the wind were her constant companion. In a two-day sail of 130 miles, *San Salvador* reached the southern edge of the magnificent bay of Magdalena. She sheltered there for four days behind the rugged,

The southern coastline of Baja California was a barren, dry realm of scrub brush and cactus that in no way resembled the lush tropical beaches of *San Salvador's* **Guatemala or the earthly paradise of the fictional island of California.**

*Courtesy
Harry Crosby*

San Salvador ◆ *Cabrillo's Galleon of Discovery*

chiseled Punta de la Trinidad to await the easing of stiff northwest winds. Long curving peninsulas of gleaming sand defined the bay beyond for the explorers and, at the entrance of the bay, rip currents formed their own cresting waves.

It was obvious that both Cabrillo and his master pilot, Ferrer, were acquainted with the charts or rutters of both their Baja California predecessors, Ulloa and Bolaños. *San Salvador* made rapid progress up the coast and Cabrillo did not tarry to provide names for landmarks already bestowed, but quickly applied his own when no preexisting titles existed. This courtesy would not be continued with Cabrillo's successor, Sebastián Vizcaíno, who sixty years later largely supplanted Cabrillo's work with a host of new place names for the California coast.

The gentle warmth of perpetual summer now highlighted *San Salvador's* sailing days. On July 19, the fleet anchored one hundred miles north of Magdalena Bay at Punta San Juanico. Here, jagged mountain peaks nicked the distant horizon at every dawn, and another headland provided *San Salvador* an excellent lee from the ever-present northwesterly winds. The rocks of this land held a reddish tint, the landscape remained arid, and mesquite and scrub dominated. The next day's log recorded progress of only fourteen miles against a stiff headwind, while *San Salvador* again tucked in behind a low headland for a night's anchorage.

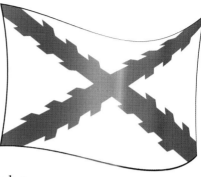

Sailing crews worked hard in Cabrillo's time, manually managing sails made of heavy flax or cloth, and lines made of hemp and other natural fibers. *San Salvador's* basic crew of sailors probably numbered fewer than thirty men – all tough, independent, prime seamen. They favored loose, baggy clothes and a belt to conveniently carry shipboard tools. Their outfits were full in the arms and legs to protect against the sun while not restricting movement aloft into the ship's rigging. Sailors almost always wore a hat of some sort to protect against the intense sunlight at sea, but their skin and complexion still reflected long days of exposure.

Cabrillo lodged in the main cabin with the pilot, with the chaplain also lodging nearby. Minor officers aboard *San Salvador* slept among the mariners. Seamen of the crew found space in the forward parts of the quarterdeck or on the lower deck from the mainmast to the poop deck. Apprentice seamen resided between the seamen and the forecastle, while young pages searched for any space left over. Bathroom facilities and indoor plumbing were non-existent, although a rough-hewn hole at the bow of the ship was used as a toilet where the flow of water would naturally clean the area.

The Cross of Burgundy flag, with a red cross on a white field, was used as a Spanish naval ensign in the sixteenth century, as well as the flag of the Viceroy of New Spain.

San Salvador ◆ *Cabrillo's Galleon of Discovery*

As *captain-general*, Cabrillo formally named a ship's master, or *maestre*, with the responsibility for sailing the vessel in consultation with the pilot, who held the duty for laying the course. Among the other ship's officers, the *contramaestre* assisted the master with the cargo and stores, held the standing of a boatswain, and directed a less senior assistant, the *guardián*.

An ordinary sailor's day followed a steady shipboard rhythm. Sailors kept busy with a daily routine that included repairing rigging or sails, cleaning decks, tarring standing rigging, or manually pumping. Following age-old seafaring tradition, those involved with handling the ship were divided into watches of eight hours (or four-hour watches twice per day). Young pages helped regulate the watch routine by chanting prayers and turning the half-hour sand clock that kept time at sea. Daily shipboard ritual featured frequent religious ceremonies especially linked to the feasts and memorials of the Spanish religious calendar. Amusements included choral singing accompanied by guitars, amateur theatricals, and various games of chance featuring cards or dice.

The majority of those onboard *San Salvador* were not, strictly speaking, sailors at all, but included soldiers, gunners, a priest, carpenters, sailmakers, scribes, caulkers, a barber-surgeon, apprentices, cooks, black slaves, those caring for the animals, and Indians. Many Spanish ships also routinely employed a diver for repairs. All were needed for the proper operation of the ship but, of course, all had to be billeted, cared for, and fed in the limited space aboard. *San Salvador's* total population probably included about one hundred individuals.

One of Cabrillo's early decisions emphasized living off the land and sea. Rather than carry an inordinate amount of ship's stores, *San Salvador* would be replenished with water and fresh food from the lands that she passed. Although this required more frequent shore parties, it also provided *San Salvador* a healthier crew.

The most important parts of the daily fare on Spanish ships included biscuit (generally one pound and a half each day) and wine (half an *azumbre* or about two pints). Biscuits were rock-hard, baked from flour and water into a cracker that could be kept edible for months. They were not eaten directly at times, but were soaked in water creating a kind of porridge.

Several days a week, a seaman's diet also included salt pork or fresh meat and rations of fish. Food was cooked in a portable wood-burning stove brought up on deck for fire safety. When the seas were too rough for cooking fires, cheese with biscuit became the common fare. With Cabrillo's penchant for fresh provisions, many scavenging parties ventured ashore and returned with game and native fruits and vegetables.

Furthermore, *San Salvador* had the good fortune to sail through one of the world's premier fishing grounds with oceanic upwelling from the cold California current, a friendly companion throughout the voyage. The success of frequent (sometimes daily) fishing efforts were often found touted in the expedition's diary.

On July 25, the *San Salvador* anchored in a large bay that Cabrillo named Puerto de Santiago after St. James the Apostle, whose feast day it was. With religious feast days on nearly every day of the Spanish calendar, this became a common naming tradition for a whole host of rich and graceful names that adorn the California coastline. A long finger of land near this harbor, Punta Abreojos, marked the farthest point north reached by the ill-fated Bolaños expedition. Good fishing ensued, but dangerous reef-strewn waters forced *San Salvador* to hurry on her progress north.

A prominent bay fifty miles north at Asunción held a surprise for the expedition – the first trees observed on the Baja California peninsula – high atop a nearby mountain. Again, *San Salvador* did not stay long. Two farther headlands were visible to the north, giving the fleet protection from the prevailing winds as it made its way farther up the coast.

While in proximity to land and now with no detailed charts of the coastline, night transits became impossible. For safety, *San Salvador* quickly developed a new daily routine that stayed with her for the entire voyage.

During the afternoon, with the winds regularly building, the ever-vigilant Cabrillo kept a lookout for a lee anchorage behind the safety of a headland. *San Salvador* then painstakingly approached shallower water with a sailor manning the sounding line and with sailors in the tops as extra lookouts, while others were poised to change sails or drop the anchor. Early the next day, after a night of relative security lying at single anchor, *San Salvador* weighed anchor and let the light land breeze of morning push her comfortably seaward to continue the northward journey. *San Salvador's* reported progress was relatively rapid using these techniques, despite confronting both prevailing winds and current at the bow.

Those aboard *San Salvador* did not know of the California current, but it was a huge factor that consistently impeded the

Along an unknown and uncharted coast, *San Salvador* **depended on her lookouts to spot hazards to navigation – rocks, shoal water, the run of the coastline – and, even, wildlife for fishing. From the ship's masthead, a lookout could see some 12-15 miles ahead on a clear day.**

Courtesy Naval Architect Doug Sharp, Sharp Design

63

San Salvador ◆ Cabrillo's Galleon of Discovery

ship's progress day after day for its entire voyage to the north. In oceanographic terms, the California current is the cold eastern portion of the vast Pacific-wide current gyre that dominates in northern latitudes. Wide and consistent, the Californian current flows from Oregon toward the Equator. The speed of the current is not as impressive as the Gulf Stream, providing no more than an average of one knot of southerly drift. Unfortunately for *San Salvador*, though, the California current displays a late-summer annual peak exactly at the time the ship faced it off the Baja California peninsula.

By August 5, the fleet had reached one of the most significant points along the entire Baja California coast, the sharp "elbow" of Punta Eugenia formed by a mountain spine of over a thousand feet that juts well out to the west. Just beyond the point is the large island of Cedros with its tall cedars and pines. Once around the point, the white-flecked, pure blue sea opened up into what Cabrillo termed "a great ensenada," with the

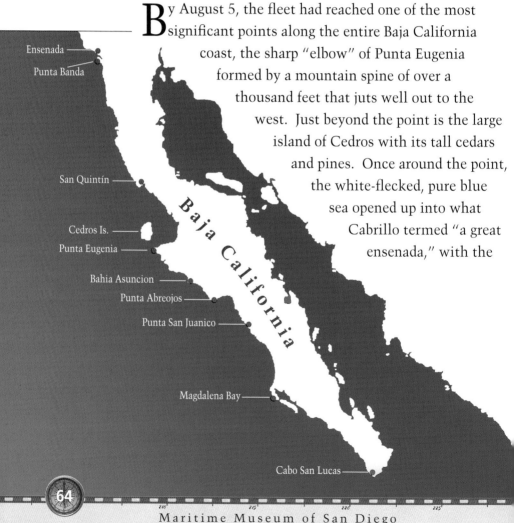

Ensenada
Punta Banda
San Quintín
Cedros Is.
Punta Eugenia
Bahia Asuncion
Punta Abreojos
Punta San Juanico
Magdalena Bay
Cabo San Lucas

Baja California

coastline disappearing from view in the distance. It was a good opportunity for *San Salvador* to pause for watering and gathering wood, and Cabrillo noted that the fishing was extremely productive in the large beds of nearby kelp.

When they again regained the California coast on August 11, 1542, the expedition discovered their first indigenous peoples of the voyage, who immediately fled inland. Cabrillo noted that the country was less rugged, although still dry and barren, with attractive plains and valleys. By August 20, *San Salvador* had anchored in the lee of Punta del Engaño, the supposed furthest point reached by Ulloa in his explorations. Only the limitless unknown lay beyond. Cabrillo's nautical charts and rutters stood open and blank before him, ready for the trove of new information to be added.

During the next day, *San Salvador* stood northward for an additional twenty-seven miles to a point of land near San Quintín, where an enclosed lagoon opened to form three distinctive arms. Cabrillo went ashore and performed a formal ceremony of possession, his first of the voyage. He claimed this "newly discovered land in the name of His Majesty and the most illustrious Don Antonio de Mendoza," and named the land Puerto de la Posesión. These formal ceremonies, which Cabrillo conducted at a dozen different locations as he steadily progressed northward, featured rich and symbolic Spanish tradition. Each was duly recorded with great fanfare in the logs.

San Salvador ◆ *Cabrillo's Galleon of Discovery*

It was also near San Quintín that the *San Salvador* crew detained three native fishermen who had tried to flee. With an eye toward cultivating friendly relations the Indians were soon released, richer for their experience with presents and baubles. When the crew next came across a group of natives, this time about thirty fishermen, they did not bolt, but cautiously approached the Spaniards. Later, the crew brought a boy and two Indian women back to the ship to reward them with even more gifts. The natives returned *San Salvador's* friendliness by showing the crew a fresh water spring as well as a natural saltworks ashore.

As this trusting relationship expanded, the natives told through sign language of other men with beards, dogs, cross-bows and swords just five days journey away. This was the first mention that Cabrillo recorded of such sightings but, as he would find, nearly every native band he encountered for the next six months told a similar tale.

Historians generally agree that this "first contact" that so riveted the attention of California's indigenous people was probably from a Spanish land expedition, perhaps that of Melchior Díaz. As one of Coronado's lieutenants, Díaz led a squadron of Spanish cavalry and Indian auxiliaries to the banks of the Colorado River during the fall of 1540. It is likely that this tale spread like wildfire from one Indian community to the next through the Californias. Cabrillo provided the Indians with a letter to be carried inland to any other Spaniards who might still be in the vicinity.

North of San Quintín the climate began to moderate to a more familiar Mediterranean model with less humidity, cooler evening temperatures, expanded cultivation, and a growing Native population. *San Salvador* carried at least one priest,

Fray Julián de Lescanso, an Augustinian monk. His duties included maintaining the Catholic faith among the crew, administering sacraments, and scrutinizing the crew's moral values. A sea-going priest would have been constantly on the lookout for signs of swearing, blasphemy, gambling, or scuffles among the hands.

One of the key responsibilities of an expedition priest involved establishing a positive atmosphere with the natives with an eye for converting them later to Catholicism. He would accompany landing parties ashore and would help establish a positive, friendly tone. At Puerto de Santa Maria, north of San Quintín, the explorers found a lagoon of fresh water where about forty Indians approached the landing party in a friendly and generous manner. They invited the Spaniards to a dinner of roast agave and fish, an event certain to have warmed Fray Julián's disposition.

Next along the coast, *San Salvador* sailed passed the prominent Punta Banda and the islands of Todos Santos, to reach the large bay of present-day Ensenada where Cabrillo performed another rite of possession. Each possession ceremony formally recorded the site's precise location and those aboard *San Salvador* carefully worked to provide a navigational location for the log.

The quadrant was used for navigation. Holding the quadrant by its ring, a star or the sun was viewed along a sight, while a second person recorded a reading of the star's altitude measured by a suspended plumb bob.

Quadrant

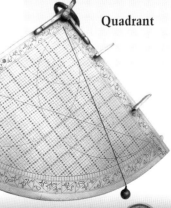

Open-ocean navigation of the time was rudimentary and most ship's masters preferred the accuracy of sailing along a known coastline or in a known direction. Coastal navigation was like navigation along a river in many ways, finding your way from port, to cape, to port.

Navigational instruments aboard *San Salvador* would have included an astrolabe, magnetic compass, a lodestone for magnetizing the compass needle, an hourglass sand clock, and a means for marking course and distance made good. The marine sand glass that was used to keep time at sea, actually used crushed eggshell rather than sand that would cling to the sides of the glass. Charts of the day had conspicuous wind roses or compass roses showing the orientation of landmasses to the 32 points of the mariner's compass. Knowing the direction of the ship's motion with the winds and using the compass rose, even an inexperienced pilot could create rough directions and plot courses to be followed.

The theories and practices of sea-going navigation during the sixteenth century, unfortunately, depended on knowledge of the Earth and the heavens that was flawed and incomplete. Navigational results, though, could be surprisingly accurate if observations were skillfully obtained and mathematical calculations correctly applied.

Everything depended on the skills of the pilot who would need to combine basic principles of science with

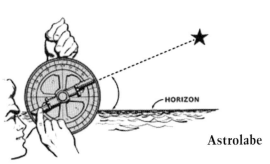

Astrolabe

technique and craft obtained through years of sea-going experience. In many ways, Spanish navigational practices of the sixteenth century led the world with royal guidelines that required pilots to obtain at-sea experience and be examined for formal certification.

The most accurate navigation technique in 1542 was to determine latitude by measuring the altitude of the sun at local noon or the height of the North Star. Navigators depended heavily on latitude to determine position, since the lack of a precise timepiece prevented an accurate determination of longitude. The sun's altitude came from a quadrant (with a plumb bob) or perhaps an astrolabe, by carefully aiming one side of the instrument at the sun and aligning the other side to a point on the horizon. Spanish pilots then used tables keyed

Navigation aboard *San Salvador* **was aided by the use of a quadrant, a mariner's astrolabe and a magnetic compass. The astrolabe was used to measure the altitude of a celestial body above the horizon to calculate latitude. These instruments were usually made of heavy brass to help steady them for use on a ship's deck.**

to the days of religious feasts that showed the noonday sun relative to the horizon at different times of the year. Converting the measured angle of the sun with these tables provided latitude.

The next most accurate navigation technique for the pilot involved dead reckoning. Here, the magnetic compass provided direction, while hand-thrown scraps, timed by heartbeat between two marks on the side of the ship and logged onto a traverse board, measured distances. With these observations of direction plus distance, a ship's track could be plotted and new "estimated positions" calculated.

Cabrillo, Ferrer, and the expedition's apprentice pilots collectively proved to be capable navigators. Voyage records show that Cabrillo and his pilots were meticulous tacticians and their observations were carefully collected and diligently recorded. Most of the positions recorded by the expedition, though, were consistently one to one-and-a-half degrees too high in latitude (about 60 – 100 nautical miles); this may not seem like a large error, but Spanish navigation, even in the

The original concept of the magnetic compass has been credited to both the Chinese and the Arabs, but its impact on Europe was immense, helping to ignite the European Renaissance, and it encouraged the growth of tremendous wealth through the expansion of European empires overseas.

early sixteenth century, routinely provided latitude estimates of much higher accuracy. This inconsistency, in an otherwise solid navigational effort, has always troubled historians. It is probable that these regular errors reflect a calibration or equipment-setting irregularity of some type. Some historians also believe that the expedition suffered from a mistake in correcting the compass' magnetic variation (possibly calibrating the compass based on Atlantic variation rather than on Pacific variation). This mistake may have led to navigational inaccuracies as well, placing the expedition's discoveries farther to the west than actually seen. The imprecise location of the port of San Diego made it difficult for later navigators to locate its precise position.

Spanish regulations required pilots to own their own navigation instruments and be conversant with charts and position plotting. Many were formally examined on their skills before assuming a titled position. Many also maintained personal rutters, some of which were state controlled and labeled as confidential.

Setting out northward again from Ensenada in favorable weather, *San Salvador* passed three uninhabited islands – the Coronado Islands, which they called *Las Islas Desiertas*. Lookouts also detected great clouds of smoke rising from ashore, deliberate fires set by the natives to clear summer brush and help germinate seeds. The voyage narrative reported: "The country appears to be good, with large valleys. Inside there are some high sierras. On the following day sailed about six leagues along a north-northwest coast and discovered a very good closed port which they named San Miguel." *San Salvador* had arrived in Alta California and the pages of her narrative contained this first European evidence of the best harbor on the southern California coast – San Diego Bay.

The easternmost of the northern Channel Islands of California, Anacapa is a long, low island that would have been seen by Cabrillo as *San Salvador* scouted the Chumash villages along the Malibu and Ventura coastlines.

Courtesy BRL Pictures

Again, a glance at the calendar of religious feasts provided the name for this discovery, *San Miguel*. This time, Cabrillo honored St. Michael's feast of September 29, the day the *captain-general* went ashore for his formal possession ceremony of this expansive bay. Three Kumeyaay greeted the Spaniards and amicably accepted gifts extended by Cabrillo. It was apparent that both parties strived for friendly relations despite a misunderstanding that had led to the wounding of three Spaniards by Indian arrows. The natives again repeated the tale of men with beards and crossbows who had killed many natives.

San Salvador stayed at San Miguel for the

next several days and with each day Cabrillo became more impressed. The crew explored the bay and continued to interact with the attentive natives including tribal women and children. The ships weathered a "great tempest" that struck the coast – the greatest they had seen on the voyage to that date, but one for which the ships were well protected inside the bay. *San Salvador* departed on October 3 after five days, and continued north along the coast witnessing "broad savannahs" and more smoke ashore.

Three days later, those aboard *San Salvador* spotted the first of the California Channel Islands and landed at Santa Catalina, probably at Avalon harbor. Cabrillo named the island after his flagship, and a second island in the distance (probably San Clemente) after *Victoria*.

Santa Cruz Island, looking much like it did to Cabrillo in 1542, is the largest of the Channel Islands. *San Salvador* **frequently sailed among these islands seeking an anchorage or a calm lee from wind and weather.**

Courtesy BRL Pictures

San Salvador ◆ *Cabrillo's Galleon of Discovery*

Again, the Spaniards encountered natives who, at first, were cautious and wary but then became cooperative. At one point the Indians rowed a "fine canoe" (with eight or ten Indians) out to the ships and accepted gifts from the *San Salvador* crew.

The ships then sailed across the channel to reach the bay at San Pedro. Cabrillo called the area Baya de los Fumos, the Bay of Smoke, for the burning chaparral of the surrounding land. *San Salvador* sailed across Santa Monica Bay where the expedition encountered a large Chumash settlement at Point Mugu. The village made an immediate impression on the Spaniards with "large houses built much like those of New Spain," and elegant canoes (many larger than they had seen before) pulled up on the beach.

For a week, *San Salvador* coasted up the strikingly beautiful California shoreline of the Santa Barbara Channel, from Point Mugu westward to Point Conception. This was undoubtedly the highlight of the voyage. The handsome, towering mountains behind the coast and the lush valleys of the lowlands provided an enticing setting. Sprinkled throughout the official voyage summary are quotes like: "a beautiful valley," "very good plains," "many groves and savannahs," "inland there are many villages and much food," and "the land appears to be very excellent."

Across the crystal blue water lay the Channel Islands, a long chain of islands rising hazy gray-green and picturesque in the distance. A warm and clear fall was in the air and, at every turn, the natives welcomed the expedition in an inquisitive and friendly manner. Alerted in advance of *San Salvador's* approach, the Indians acted in the same comfortable and non-threatening manner shown by the Spaniards. They readily bartered with fresh fish, sardines, berries and healthy local foods.

The voyage's chronicler listed many different villages along the coast by their Indian names. This was an indication of the friendly nature of the interaction, the presence of a large

The rugged and wave-tossed coastline of San Miguel Island belies the fact that it boasts the best-protected bay among the Channel Islands, Cuyler Harbor. *San Salvador* **found protection here on several occasions and it is believed by some to be where Cabrillo suffered the accidental fall, which caused the injury that ultimately killed him.**
Courtesy BRL Pictures

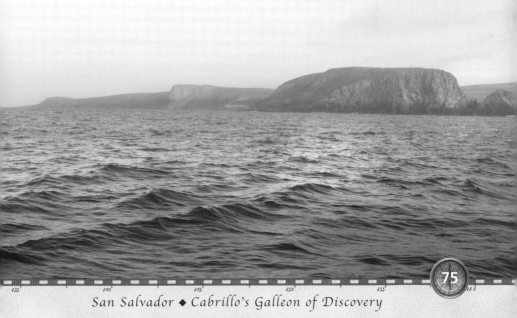

San Salvador ◆ *Cabrillo's Galleon of Discovery*

population, and the region's abundant food supply. As the crews traded iron products, nails, and cloth for water and a wide variety of fresh foods, native canoes often accompanied the ships as they moved farther up the coast. Cabrillo was so confident of the natives' friendship that, for the first time, he allowed the ships of the fleet to scatter in their visits to different villages and offshore islands.

Cabrillo next resolved to round Point Conception and continue north, but strong northwest winds and ocean swells, torn and white-whipped, threw him back. It was a common condition near Point Conception and Point Arguello that any modern-day mariner would know well, but for *San Salvador,* priorities shifted to finding a haven for safety. While falling off to the southeast, the Spaniards discovered San Miguel Island, the most westerly of the

San Salvador **carried at least one longboat, probably secured on the forecastle or at the waist and, at times, towed astern. It was used in landings on the beach, in the reconnaissance of bays or shallow areas, or in the transport of men and supplies between the ships of the expedition.**

Drawing by Jack Williams

Channel Islands. Here was exactly the sheltering harbor they sought, notched into the northeast side of the island.

San Salvador waited windbound for eight days at San Miguel. The snug confines of the harbor protected her nicely from west and northwest winds, but the narrow channel was the very devil to navigate during a storm. When she finally stood out to sea, *San Salvador* headed northward again toward Point Conception in search of a wide river mentioned by the natives.

This time a winter storm brought strong southeasterly winds. Cabrillo took immediate advantage of the wind shift to surge rapidly northward up the coast. *San Salvador* stayed well out to sea for safety, but as conditions worsened in blowing overcast and spray, *Victoria* disappeared from view.

San Salvador probably made landfall at Point Reyes, just north of San Francisco Bay, and continued up the coast until reaching a location near the Russian River. She then turned south in search of her consort, missing the entrance to San Francisco Bay, but finding *Victoria* safely at anchor repairing storm damage. Continuing south Cabrillo identified Monterey Bay, noting mountains and trees covered with snow. Beating around Cypress Point, *San Salvador* coasted along Big Sur, where "the mountains seem to reach the heavens and the sea beats on them; sailing close to land, it appears as though they would fall on the ships. They are covered with snow to the summits." Stern winds and cresting seas pushed the ship rapidly down the coast. The expedition reached either San Miguel Island or Santa Rosa Island by November 23 with the intent to winter there.

It was here that Juan Rodríguez Cabrillo met his end on January 3, 1543, following an accidental fall that resulted in a broken leg or arm. It was said that he was jumping ashore from a small boat while responding to an Indian attack on a small Spanish shore party. Before he died, Cabrillo formally named Bartolomé Ferrer as *captain-general* of the expedition and specifically directed him to continue to explore the California coast. The narrative of the voyage records Cabrillo's burial on the island of Capitana, "because he died there the island retained the name Capitana."

T he exact location of Cabrillo's burial is unknown. In 1901, though, a cryptic stone artifact came to light on Santa Rosa Island that some claim is Cabrillo's headstone. The slab-sided sandstone relic is about fourteen inches in length and contains the initials "JR" below a cross and a stick figure of a headless man. The authenticity of the relic remains unproven, but does draw attention to the adventurous life that Cabrillo led.

This slabstone, found in an Indian midden on Santa Rosa Island in 1901, is believed by some to be the grave marker for Juan Rodríguez Cabrillo, who died after an accidental fall. Its authenticity is open to much speculation despite the presence of the hand-carved initials "JR", a cross and a headless figure.

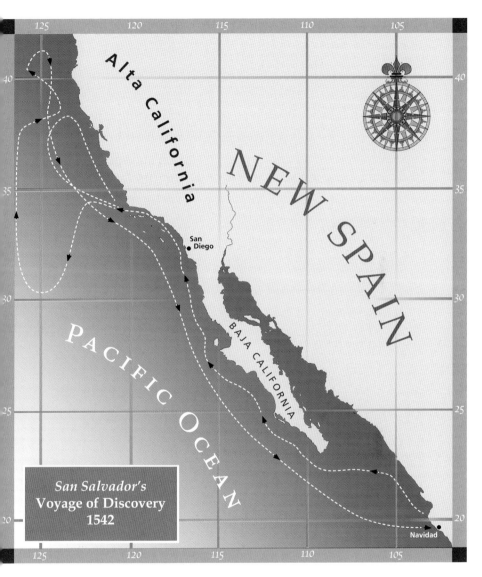

San Salvador's
Voyage of Discovery
1542

In February 1543, Ferrer sailed first from Santa Cruz Island
to the mainland for fresh provisions and then took the
fleet boldly northward. His intention was not to stay close
to the coast, as Cabrillo had done, but to sail several days out

San Salvador ◆ Cabrillo's Galleon of Discovery

to sea until he had reached the latitude of Point Reyes and then to close the coast and continue northward. He sailed seaward for about 300 miles and then, catching easterly and southeasterly winds, the fleet swung to the north and then finally back toward the shore. Despite the long distances sailed, *San Salvador* made a perfect landfall at Point Reyes – certainly a reflection of Ferrer's navigational skills.

Without skipping a beat, Ferrer directed *San Salvador* farther up the coast probably to Point Arena. He then turned to the northwest and opened the coastline in strong winds that pushed *San Salvador* briskly ahead. Historians speculate that Ferrer's plan of leaving the coast at this time matched the overall prediction that the North American coastline would begin to curve to the west toward the Orient. Whatever the reason, the ships reached the approximate latitude of the present day California-Oregon border in just four days before fog, sleet, blowing snow, and southwest winds "of great fury" turned them back.

The fleet now labored within the grip of a severe Pacific winter storm, several hundred miles off the coast, which would test *San Salvador's* rugged construction to its limits. There was little the crews could do but hold on as winds and the cold, heaving sea battered the ships. The seas were confused, coming from different directions and, with a low forecastle, the seas could easily break over the bow taking green water aboard. *San Salvador* repeatedly

A severe Pacific winter storm, known to anyone who has sailed off the Pacific northwest coast, finally spelled the end for the battered expedition at its most northerly point, approximately at today's California-Oregon border.

Painting by Richard DeRosset, MMSD Collections

RICHARD DEROSSET ®

San Salvador ◆ Cabrillo's Galleon of Discovery

lurched frighteningly to leeward, and then crashed down into the hollows of a confused turmoil of sea. At one point, the only course for survival was to run, or "scud," to the northeast before the gale – a perilous choice with the threat of running out of sea room and grounding if, in fact, the coastline was bending to the west. This fear intensified as birds and fresh logs were seen, an indication certainly of approaching land. Storm waves climbed still higher in the shifting winds at the core of a strong low-pressure system. The winds then veered sharply to the north accompanied by strong rain and falling temperatures as the storm front passed them. Battered, nearly out of control and with little choice, Ferrer ordered *San Salvador* and *Victoria* back toward the southeast and Point Reyes.

Beaten back from the mark of their greatest advance to the north or west, the exhausted crew continued southward seeking a safe harbor for repairs and recuperation. With the zephyr now laying at their back, *San Salvador* flew southeastward sailing broadly from Point Reyes to the Channel Islands in a mere forty hours. High breaking seas blocked the narrow harbor entrance off San Miguel and the ship continued on to a protected anchorage at Santa Cruz Island, arriving on March 5, 1543.

With the ships storm-beaten and leaking, Ferrer made the logical conclusion that a return to New Spain with all of the expedition's discoveries, logs, and geographical knowledge intact was the best course of action. With both ship and crew spent, *San Salvador* retraced her steps back through the Channel Islands to San Diego. There, she stayed almost a week. When she resumed her return voyage, her crew contained two new passengers – Indian boys to be trained as interpreters for returning voyagers.

Victoria had disappeared from view in stormy weather near Santa Cruz Island, but as *San Salvador* approached Isle de Cedros on the Baja California coast, she appeared improbably on the distant horizon. The reunion was joyous as both crews were certain that the other had been lost. With the gentle wind and current in their favor, the expedition's ships arrived back at Navidad on April 14, 1543, nearly ten months after departing.

The remaining years of *San Salvador's* service are yet to be discovered. It is widely believed that Viceroy Mendoza included the ship with others he organized in late 1543 for trade with Peru. This decision did not bode well for *San Salvador*, as conditions in Peru were chaotic. Many ships sent on Peruvian trading ventures during this era never returned to New Spain.

For *San Salvador*, the last pages of her history are blank. She may have been overwhelmed one pitch-black night by tall and wicked waves, her last minutes filled with the sounds of grinding timber and roaring winds as solid water poured over her decks. She may just have simply and quietly disappeared from view one day in the great, gray immensity of the Pacific, or she may have died slowly and wistfully while abandoned and worm-eaten in an obscure Central American inlet. We do not know where she sailed, what new coastlines she traced, or what new islands she charted. No account of *San Salvador's* ultimate fate has survived.

San Salvador ◆ *Cabrillo's Galleon of Discovery*

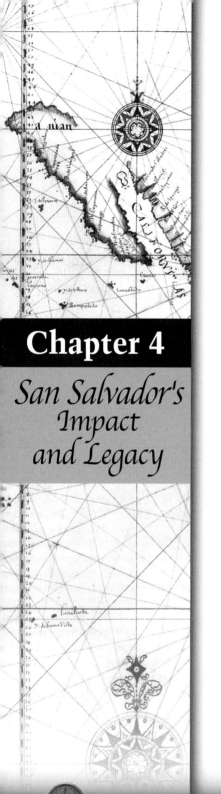

Chapter 4

San Salvador's Impact and Legacy

G rateful for their safe return to Navidad and for the skill of their commanders, most men of *San Salvador* were simply happy to give thanks for their salvation and celebrate their reunion with friends and family. Tales were told of towering seas, mighty winds, and enticing new lands. Cartographers dug through treasure troves of new knowledge and priests dreamed of bringing the Faith to new peoples. For Viceroy Antonio de Mendoza, though, it was quite a different story.

After investing a fortune to outfit his twin sea-going expeditions of discovery, Viceroy Mendoza faced a grim reality: one expedition had disappeared off the edge of the map and the second had returned battered and without its *captain-general*. Worse, Cabrillo's expedition discovered no great fortune, no magical strait to the Atlantic, and no route to the Orient.

Mendoza seemed star-crossed; all three of his mighty expeditions as viceroy had come to naught. *San Salvador* brought no pearls, gold, spices, nor word of Villalobos. Villalobos himself found no return route to New Spain and eventually died in the Philippines. Coronado's exploration in the American southwest returned with no riches from the rumored northern cities of gold. In a colonial society that prized conquest, exploration, and territorial expansion as the means for the growth of personal and imperial wealth, Mendoza had struck out after three swings. Mendoza was transferred to Peru as viceroy where he died just one year later, while Luis de Velasco stepped in as the Crown's viceroy in New Spain.

With the lack of riches from the Cabrillo expedition and the departure of Mendoza, further plans for California exploration were suspended. No further funding from the Crown could be expected, or private investment seeking an ambitious return. In fact, at the time no one could think of any pressing need for another California expedition.

For Europeans the golden potential of California soon faded. For indigenous Californians, the rise toward a new multicultural society would wait for a later day. The viceroy of New Spain redirected energies toward that which could create wealth and fame: precious metals from Peruvian mines, exotic riches from Oriental trade, and profits from an exploited population. His priorities were immediate and near-term. Expansion of empire and its defense where no other competition existed waited for another day.

San Salvador's legacy is complex, as the bounty from the voyage was not immediately obvious to those who chronicled its accomplishments. *San Salvador's* explorations did not lead to speedy conquests, immense fortunes, or benefits to those who sailed aboard her. But the longer she is studied, the more her true impact comes into clearer focus.

Spanish explorers relied on their mastery of the sea to maintain their New World conquests and to make these economically worthy. Spanish seafarers employed some of the most complex sailing machines yet invented, their navigators carefully surveyed the shores they discovered, and their pilots solved the secrets of the great wind and current systems of the oceans. *San Salvador* contributed greatly in each of these realms, and it is here that historians have bestowed their most lavish praise five hundred years later.

Although no California gold flowed to the Spanish court, Cabrillo's postscript was written in a hundred other ways. *San Salvador* created the footing upon which later Spanish explorers of the Pacific stood, she enhanced Spanish claims in North America, and she extended Spanish mastery over Pacific seas. The galleon's logs overflowed with thousands of details of coastlines, bays, mountains, islands, winds and weather. With *San Salvador* reaching lands that no European had ever seen, the world's mapmakers pushed back the unknown for nearly a thousand miles and transformed the fabled land of California from myth into reality. Native societies, undisturbed by European ways, were described in detail and the interaction between Spaniard and Indian provided a documentation of cultures in transition.

After 1543, Spanish priorities for Pacific exploration shifted toward its settlement of the Philippine Islands, opening a gateway to China and to the Orient, and trading in spices. This approach made economic sense,

much more than any venture in California. The immediate challenge and priority for Spain became the need for a true two-way trans-pacific route between New Spain and the Indies.

Here *San Salvador's* legacy again came to the fore, as Spanish trade to the Orient depended on cracking the code of Pacific winds that would speed Spanish ships on their way. Spanish mariners such as Magellan, Loaísa, and Saavedra had found an efficient track westward across the Pacific aided by the wide belt of the northeast trade winds just north of the equator. Once in the western Pacific, though, no return

An iconic view of the classic galleon or carrack design by Flemish Renaissance painter, Pieter Bruegel, the Elder, c.1560.

San Salvador ◆ *Cabrillo's Galleon of Discovery*

path could be found back to New Spain. Attempts to sail eastward meant battling adverse winds, and any route farther westward encroached upon Portuguese claims where the Spaniards were restricted by international treaties. Spanish explorers had to find a way back across the Pacific in order to profit from any trade with China.

The first real break in solving this mystery came from famed Spanish pilot and navigator Andrés de Urdaneta.   From his time with the Loaísa Pacific expedition of 1525, Urdaneta had already gained some knowledge of Pacific winds. As he also prepared the formal narrative report of Cabrillo's voyage in 1543, Urdaneta obtained access to the extensive logs and charts of the Cabrillo

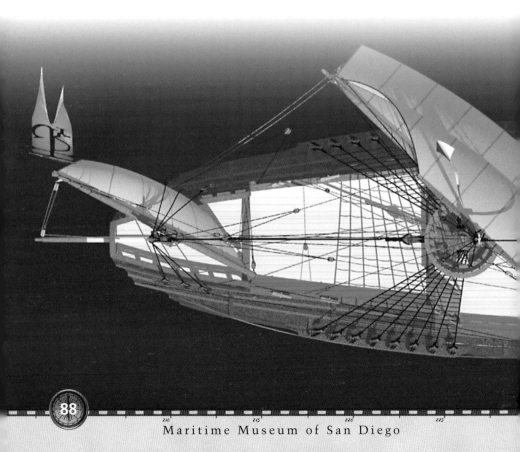

expedition with their recordings of winds and weather. From these experiences, Urdaneta strengthened the belief and theory that ocean winds flowed to the east in the far northern latitudes of the Pacific. Even more important for Pacific voyaging, he could now suggest the best season of the year to conduct a return sail.

Urdaneta joined the Legaspi expedition to the Philippines in 1564-1565, and successfully piloted the galleon *San Pedro* back to New Spain by first sailing far to the north. Urdaneta crossed the Pacific toward New Spain with the prevailing westerlies and then turned southeast short of the coast. With the winds at his back, he made landfall on San Miguel Island, just south of Point Conception. It was clear Urdaneta used Cabrillo's charts including his reference

Courtesy Naval Architect Doug Sharp, Sharp Design

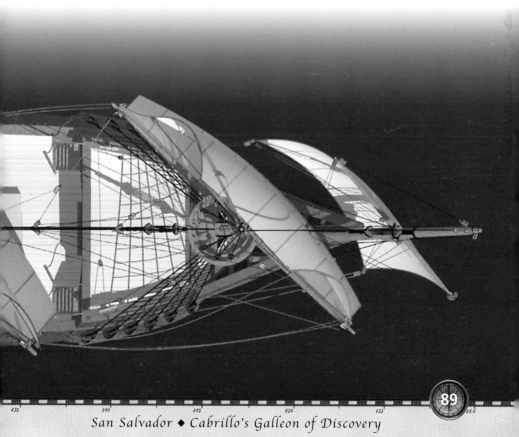

San Salvador ◆ *Cabrillo's Galleon of Discovery*

to the island as "San Salvador," in a ghostly reference to Cabrillo's great ship. *San Pedro* arrived safely in Acapulco four months after leaving the Philippines, and the new trans-Pacific track quickly gained recognition as "Urdaneta's Route".

Urdaneta's Route became the longest regular trade route of the age, the annual cycle of the Manila galleons that brought Oriental treasure back to New Spain and then trans-shipped it directly to Europe – the dream of Christopher Columbus. Not only had Cabrillo's discoveries helped solve the riddle of the Pacific winds, but his careful charting of the California coast provided the navigational details, especially in latitude, that Manila galleons needed to shape their course to Navidad or Acapulco. With the help of the *San Salvador's* logs, the return route of the Manila galleons would almost exactly match what, today, we consider the most efficient cross-Pacific sailing route – that of the Great Circle.

San Salvador discoveries influenced, in some manner, each of the few Spanish voyages that sailed to California for the next two hundred years. Both the exploratory voyages of Pedro de Unamuno (who touched at Morro Bay in 1587) and Sebastián Rodríguez Cermeño (who explored in the vicinity of Drake's Bay in 1595) sailed to California by following Urdaneta's Route from the Philippines and used Cabrillo's charts to guide their efforts along the coast. In 1602 and 1603, Sebastián Vizcaíno led an exploring expedition of three ships in a quest to discover a port suitable as a haven for eastbound Manila galleons. Vizcaíno retraced Cabrillo's route almost exactly from New Spain, across the Gulf of California, up the Baja California coast and as high as the Oregon border in Alta California. He renamed the port of San Miguel, San Diego de Alcalá, in honor of the feast day of his arrival.

San Salvador's voyage of exploration is usually viewed today in isolation, the sailing of two small ships up an unknown coast. In reality, though, the early sixteenth century in North America was alive with tales of exploration, discoveries, and advances in knowledge, geography, and science that sparkled across every decade. *San Salvador* established a high-water mark of exploration along the West Coast, but her accomplishments were greatly aided by others. Much like American spacefaring, her voyage built on the success of expeditions that immediately preceded her, each inching the mark further forward until *San Salvador* could finally apply a voyager's footprints to the beaches of today's California. If the *San Salvador* expedition represented the Apollo 11 mission of her day, then the northward voyages of Ulloa, Alarcón, and Bolaños embodied the Mercury and Gemini predecessors of the main event.

San Salvador's voyage was not just an isolated footnote of American history, as some view it. It stands as the West Coast component of a larger story that stretched across the entire American continent. The Spanish imperial system rewarded land, power, and esteem to those exploring into the unknown and extending Spanish claims. Motivated by sagas of gold and fortune, sixteenth-century Spanish expeditions across America were wide-ranging and spawned expansion and settlement.

Seen in this light, *San Salvador* supplies a Pacific mirror-image to what has always been an Atlantic-centric view of "American" history. *San Salvador's* 1542 voyage of discovery up the coast of an unknown California relates favorably with other European voyages of discovery along the unknown east coast of North America, which occurred during the same era.

The first comparable voyage of exploration along the U. S. east coast occurred but thirty years before *San Salvador,* with Ponce de León sailing northward to discover an unusually strong current

San Salvador ◆ *Cabrillo's Galleon of Discovery*

(the Gulf Stream) and the virgin shores of Florida. Hernando de Soto's expedition through Florida, Georgia, and to the Mississippi River occurred during the same years as Cabrillo's voyage, and the first permanent European settlement in the continental United States (in St. Augustine) did not occur until twenty years after *San Salvador's* return. As a point of comparison, the first permanent English settlement at Jamestown did not come until 1607, two generations after Juan Rodríguez Cabrillo's death. Defining the coastline of what would become the United States, interacting with its indigenous peoples, and planning for a new future did not have to wait for the voyage

Maritime Museum of San Diego

of the *Susan Constant* to Virginia in 1607, or the voyage of the *Mayflower* to Plymouth in 1621; it was alive in the contributions to history that *San Salvador* provided.

It was through navigation and maps that *San Salvador* may have provided her greatest contribution to the flow of history. Despite inaccuracies in the plotting of specific latitudes and global positions, the expedition's records, logs and sightings provided a first time appreciation of a part of the world that had never been recorded on a map before. Using the science of cartography,

These Kumeyaay rock drawings were discovered in San Diego's East County and appear to represent two or three European ships with masts, sails, and (possibly) an anchor. The rock petroglphs estimated age could place them at the time of the early Spanish expeditions and, possibly, they could be the sole surviving representation of Cabrillo's ships.
MMSD Collections

Europeans created maps and charts to help better understand distant lands once unknown. These charts also became a powerful tool of European imperialists who helped define, defend and partition the world's available lands into colonial spheres, and certainly assisted Spain in pursuing her claims of conquest throughout the Pacific that proliferated with each new addition to the mapmaker's library.

Although no Spanish painting, or even a definitive description of *San Salvador* survived the centuries, one may yet exist. Ironically, this illustration exists not through the efforts of a European painter, but through the energies of a Kumeyaay artisan near San Diego.

For thousands of years, and predating the first kingdoms of Egypt, the Kumeyaay occupied broad areas of Southern California and Baja California, while depending on the sea for sustenance and livelihood. In many ways their local cultural roots and continuity of their language ranked as some of the longest in history. Further north elaborate canoes and extensive boatbuilding also distinguished the Chumash people of the Channel Islands and the California mainland. These Native peoples had developed maritime knowledge and traditions, built permanent dwellings along bays and seashores, and had boats for fishing and offshore travel. They also left petroglyphs on rock faces throughout Southern California describing elements of their lives.

Despite this knowledge of the sea and boats, the arrival of large Spanish vessels with their enormous expanse of masts and sails, colorful banners, large crews, cannon, and firearms would have made a stunning impact on the native culture. Cabrillo noted in his voyage records that Indians throughout California had repeated nearly identical tales of Spanish conquistadors, weapons, armor, horses and dogs. Although probably only referring to a single brief encounter with a Spanish land party near the Colorado River, the story of first contact with Europeans was so captivating and threatening that it spread rapidly across the entire California native population. The sudden arrival of the impressive ships of the Cabrillo expedition would have had a similar impact on native lore. Stories would have been repeated far and wide along the pathways of native oral communications.

In the backcountry of San Diego, rare Kumeyaay rock drawings have come to light that feature several stick representations of people standing next to two objects that look strikingly like sailing ships. A third smaller, but very similar object (another sailing ship?), stands nearby. Each of the "ships" appears to have a hull, masts and sails, and one ship may have what looks like a bowsprit or anchor. No captions or script tell us exactly what the drawings entail, but it is not uncommon for older societies to describe events in pictures when no native descriptive vocabulary words yet exist.

If these ship drawings portrayed an actual event, it must have been an event of significant impact – much like the oft-repeated native tale of Spaniards near the Colorado River. It might have represented any one of several ship visits, but circumstantial evidence does weigh in favor of the Cabrillo voyage. Spanish ship visits near San Diego Bay were few across a two-hundred year period. The most likely event to have captured native attention was probably the very first time such ships appeared – the Cabrillo expedition. In addition to the fact that it was the first European ship to visit Southern California shores, the expedition included multiple ships (including one much smaller than the other two), and the expedition stayed in San Diego Bay during two different stops where local Kumeyaay visited daily. Not only may this be the only surviving image of *San Salvador*, but it may also, in the words of historian Dr. Ray Ashley, "constitute the earliest primary-source graphic representation of an historic event in American history."

The immediate implications of this ancient rock drawing are many. Most important of all, though, may be that it serves to remind us of another time in California history and the profound legacy that a shipload of one hundred Spanish adventurers left at our shores nearly five hundred years ago.

San Salvador
**approaching Point Loma
and San Diego Bay.**
Painting by Gordon Miller

San Salvador ◆ Cabrillo's Galleon of Discovery

Acknowledgements

The author is deeply indebted to the original and detailed research performed by an inspiring group of researchers and academicians who have studied and tracked the intriguing story of the galleon *San Salvador* through every course change and across a history largely hidden and convoluted. It is their abundant and meticulous work that underpins the saga of *San Salvador* told here. This book represents a compendium work and the author would like to thank a host of enthusiastic historians and researchers who have led the way: Dr. Ray Ashley, Dr. Filipe Castro, Dr. Iris Engstrand, Dr. John Johnson, Dr. Harry Kelsey, Dr. W. Michael Mathes, Paul A. Myers, Pablo E. Pérez-Mallaína, Dr. Carla Rahn Phillips, Doug Sharp, Dr. Kevin Sheehan, Neva Sullaway, Dr. Michael E. Thurman, Henry Raup Wagner and Dr. Jack S. Williams.

In addition to these fine historians, many others directly contributed to the success of this important telling of the history of the first ship to sail along the California coast. Keeping in mind that neither sets of ship's plans nor pictures exist of *San Salvador*, Dr. Ray Ashley, the President & CEO of the Maritime Museum of San Diego, sponsored a unique international gathering of Spanish-era experts on shipbuilding and galleon construction to create the best consensus for the design elements for *San Salvador*. Not only were these conclusions at the core of the design of the replica *San Salvador*, built along the shores of San Diego Bay, but also provided the technical basis for this book. Dr. Ashley also conceived an exceptional voyage under sail of the topsail schooner *Californian*, with this author aboard, which vigilantly traced Juan Rodríguez Cabrillo's progress through California's Channel Islands.

Neva Sullaway, editor of the Maritime Museum of San Diego's remarkable *Mains'l Haul - A Journal of Pacific Maritime History*, offered superb editorial assistance. Ray Ashley, Iris Engstrand, and Kevin Sheehan read and reviewed the manuscript with a careful eye. Anthony Enyedy, a splendid artist in his own right, provided the book's eye-catching layout. Joanne Lee assisted with proofreading. Thanks also to artists and photographers: Gordon Miller, Richard DeRosset, Bruce Dragoo, and Maggie and Ted Walton. Roman Detyna and the designers at Digital Navy developed a marvelous paper scale model of *San Salvador* that complements this ship's history.

Sources and Suggested Reading

Many of the sources listed here were used extensively in documenting details provided in this book and all provide exciting insights into the times of *San Salvador* in the Pacific.

Ashley, Raymond E. "California's Origin Story," *Mains'l Haul: A Journal of Pacific Maritime History* (V.45:1&2, Winter/Spring 2009), 8-21.

Bleichman, Daniela and Paula De Vos, Kristin Huffine, Kevin Sheehan (ed.), *Science in the Spanish and Portuguese Empires 1500-1800* (Stanford University Press, Stanford: 2009).

Engstrand, Iris and Harry Kelsey. "Juan Rodríguez Cabrillo and the Building of the San Salvador," *Mains'l Haul: A Journal of Pacific Maritime History* (V.45:1&2, Winter/Spring 2009), 36-51.

Engstrand, Iris and Donald Cutter, *Quest for Empire: Spanish Settlement in the Southwest*. (Fulcrum Publishing, Golden, Colorado:1996).

Engstrand, Iris, *San Diego: California's Cornerstone* (Sunbelt Publications, El Cajon: 2005).

Guassac, Louis, "Kumeyaay and the Ocean," *Mains'l Haul: A Journal of Pacific Maritime History.* (V.47:1&2, Winter/spring 2011), 58-67.

Holmes, Maurice G., *From New Spain by Sea to the Californias: 1519-1668* (Arthur H. Clark, Glendale: 1963).

Kelsey, Harry, *Discovering Cabrillo* (Liber Apertus Press, Saratoga: 2004).

Kelsey, Harry, *Juan Rodríguez Cabrillo* (Huntington Library, San Marino: 1998).

Lemke, Nancy, *Cabrillo: First European Explorer of the California Coast* (EZ Nature Books, San Luis Obispo: 1991).

Mathes, W. Michael, *A Brief History of the Land of Calafia: The Californias 1533-1795* (University of San Francisco: 1977).

Mathes, W. Michael, "The Early Exploration of the Pacific Coast," North American Exploration, Volume I (University of Nebraska Press, Lincoln: 1997).

Morison, Samuel Eliot, The European Discovery of America: The Southern Voyages 1492-1616 (Oxford University Press, New York: 1974).

Myers, Paul A., North to California: The Spanish Voyages of Discovery 1533-1603 (Llumina Press, Coral Springs: 2004).

Nauman, James D. (ed.), An Account of the Voyage of Juan Rodríguez Cabrillo (Cabrillo National Monument Foundation, San Diego: 1999).

Pérez-Mallaína, Pablo E., Spain's Men of the Sea: Daily Life on the Indies Fleets in the Sixteenth Century (Johns Hopkins University Press, Baltimore: 1998).

Phillips, Carla Rahn, "Cabrillo in Context: Pacific Exploration in the Early Sixteenth Century," Mains'l Haul: A Journal of Pacific Maritime History (V.45:1&2, Winter/Spring 2009), 22-35.

Phillips, Carla Rahn, Six Galleons for the King of Spain: Imperial Defense in the Early Seventeenth Century (Johns Hopkins University Press, Baltimore: 1986).

Reupsch, Carl F. (ed.), The Cabrillo Era and his Voyage of Discovery (Cabrillo Historical Association, San Diego: 1982).

Schurz, William Lytle, The Manila Galleon EP Dutton & Co., New York: 1939).

Vernon, Edward W., A Maritime History of Baja California Viego Press, Santa Barbara, 2010).

Wagner, Henry R., Juan Rodríguez Cabrillo: Discoverer of the Coast of California (California Historical Society, San Francisco: 1941).

Wagner, Henry R., Spanish Voyages to the Northwest Coast of America in the Sixteenth Century (California Historical Society, San Francisco, 1929).

Williams, Jack S., "Alta California and Spanish Naval Strategy in the Pacific: An Overview from the 16th Century to the early 19th Century," Mains'l Haul: A Journal of Pacific Maritime History V.45:1&2, Winter/Spring 2009), 58-71.

Timeline of Early Expl

1490	1500	1510	1520	1530	1540	1550

1492
Columbus
(West Indies)

1513
Ponce de León
(Florida)

1519
Alvarez de
Pineda
(Texas)

1524
Verrazzano
(East Coast)

1539
DeSoto
(Southeast)

1540
Coronado
(Southwest)

1542
Cabrillo
(California)

1565
St. Augus
settle
(Florid

Maritime Museum of San Diego

ion in the United States

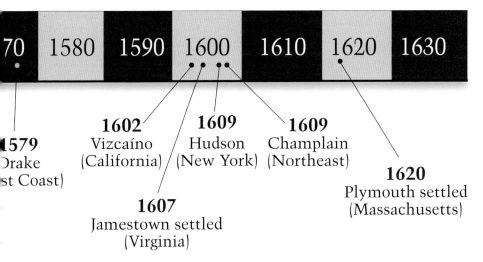

70	1580	1590	1600	1610	1620	1630

1579
Drake
st Coast)

1602
Vizcaíno
(California)

1607
Jamestown settled
(Virginia)

1609
Hudson
(New York)

1609
Champlain
(Northeast)

1620
Plymouth settled
(Massachusetts)

San Salvador ◆ *Cabrillo's Galleon of Discovery*

Teacher Resources for the Study of the *San Salvador*

The voyage of explorer Juan Rodríguez Cabrillo, along the coast of California in 1542, provides California and the United States West Coast with its origin story – the first interaction of European explorers with indigenous peoples, the first time that California was plotted on the maps of the world, and the first hint of the multi-cultural society that California would become. The study of Cabrillo and his flagship, *San Salvador*, touches on a host of subjects that stand as the cornerstone of California history and social science studies.

California History-Social Science Content Standards K-12

The study of the voyage of the *San Salvador* provides rich ground for a host of instructional subjects in history including:

- The first European exploration of the coast of California.
- The first cultural interaction between Europeans and the well-established Native people of California.
- The importance of the evolving technologies involving mathematics, astronomy, measurements in nature, navigation, map-making and weather, and how they assisted the worldwide exploration in the sixteenth century.
- The impact in California of the spread of Spanish culture, economy, and government.
- Cabrillo's voyage (1542) in the context of other explorations and settlements in the present-day U. S. including those of DeSoto, Ponce de León, Cabot, Coronado, Bering, and Hudson, and settlements in St Augustine (1565), Jamestown (1607), and Plymouth (1620).
- The study and importance of early maps showing California as an island and an unexplored Pacific ocean leading toward China and the Spice Islands.

Content Standards	*San Salvador* chapters addressing content standards
Grade 2/2.5	Chapters 1, 3
Grade 3/3.2	Chapters 3
Grade 3/3.3.1	Chapters 3
Grade 4/4.1	Chapter 3 (incl. maps)
Grade 4/4.2.1-4.2.6	Chapters 1, 3, 4
Grade 5/5.1.1	Chapters 1, 3
Grade 5/5.2	Chapters 1, 2, 3, 4
Grade 5/5.3.1, 5.3.6	Chapters 1, 3
Grade 7/7.7.1, 7.7.3	Chapters 1, 3
Grade 7/7.11.1	Chapters 3

Index

Note: **Bold brown** numbers represent illustrations, maps, photos or paintings relating to the subject matter.

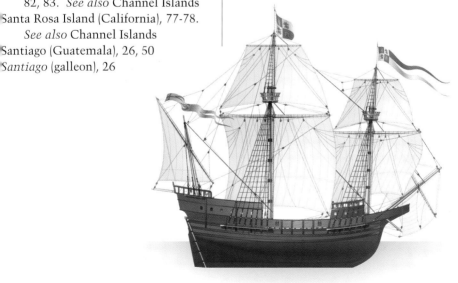

San Salvador ◆ *Cabrillo's Galleon of Discovery*

Download a paper model of *San Salvador* and enter the exciting world of ship modeling. Offered free-of-charge by the Maritime Museum of San Diego, this model will help teach young and old alike the details of sixteenth-century Spanish galleons.

The paper model is made from a series of digital design sheets that are downloaded over the Internet and printed out on paper from an ink-jet or color laser printer.

Go to the Maritime Museum's website at: www.sdmaritime.org/san-salvador-build/ for details on how to download the model's design sheets and for detailed assembly instruction

This book and other items are also available from the Maritime Museum store or online at: http://www.sdmaritime.org/shop/

Maritime Museum of San Diego

The mission of the Maritime Museum of San Diego is to serve as the community memory of our seafaring experience by collecting, preserving, and presenting our rich and diverse maritime heritage and historic connections with the Pacific world.

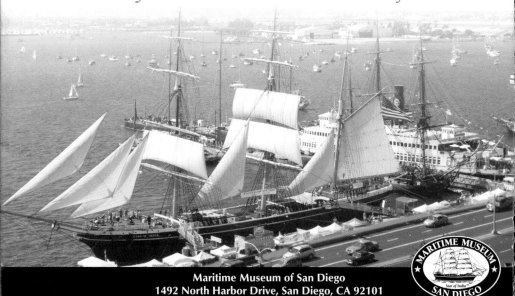

Maritime Museum of San Diego
1492 North Harbor Drive, San Diego, CA 92101
Phone: 619.234.9153 · www.sdmaritime.org